Baking French Mac␣␣␣ Guide

Written and photographed by

Lisa Maliga

Copyright © 2016

Disclaimer

This information is to demonstrate how various products can be utilized. This information is based on my own research and is believed to be accurate. The author assumes no liability for misuse of ingredients or data and urges any crafter or baker to do their own testing to ensure the ingredients meet their own specifications.

ISBN-13: 978-1539636595

ISBN-10: 1539636593

Table of Contents

CHAPTER 1

Introduction

A funny thing happened when I baked my first batch of French macarons. They didn't turn out the way I hoped they would. So I decided to make another batch. And another. And another. I wanted macarons with those ruffled edges known as feet. I wanted them to be brightly colored and light as air, and without hollows. In other words, I wanted a perfect batch of macarons. And I kept trying until I got it right.

Making a pound cake from scratch is the most advanced baking I've ever done. This dessert contains the most basic ingredients found in your pantry and fridge: eggs, butter, flour, sugar, vanilla extract and baking powder. As long as you have a hand or stand mixer and measure your ingredients correctly, it's not difficult to bake.

Macarons also require few ingredients: two types of sugar, egg whites, almond flour, and color. That's it as far as the cookies, a/k/a shells go. The fillings can be diverse: jam or jelly, caramel, Nutella, butterscotch, lemon curd, etc. You can make your own whether it's buttercream, chocolate ganache, or a fruity homemade jam.

I'd never used a piping/pastry bag before. In fact, I thought they were only used for decorating cakes and cupcakes. It took me two dozen tries to get the perfect macaron with a smooth yet slightly rounded top, little frilly feet that are the hallmark of this delicacy, and without hollow insides. The filling was scrumptious too – lemon butter curd. What's that? You'll find out as I've included the recipe.

After discovering local bakeries and stores that sold macarons, I didn't have to settle for a limited selection of colors/flavors. I didn't even have to drive to the nearest store that sold them in their freezer section. Nope, I could have fresh macarons whenever I wanted. Well, whenever I had a few hours to spare...

I took copious notes each time I baked a batch. I also took photos, though not always of every step. Still, for the past eleven months, I've learned so much and now want to share some tips and recipes with anyone who's motivated to bake these delicacies.

If you want to bake macarons, I'd recommend the three P's: preparation, patience and practice.

1] Preparation. This entails sifting your almond flour and sugar beforehand, separating your egg whites and aging them or at least having them sit out long enough to attain room temperature.

2] Patience. Each step has a reason for being there. Don't rush the meringue or macaronage process. Don't pull the macaron shells out of the oven too early or pry them off the silicone mat or parchment paper before they're ready. It means not adding filling before they've cooled off. I'll also admit that the most difficult thing about all this work that you've invested in making these little sandwich cookies is that you shouldn't eat them right away! Of course, you can, but if you wait 24 hours, they will taste a lot better.

3] Practice. Perfection or near-perfection usually doesn't happen after you make your first batch. Knowing when your meringue is at its peak, when the macaronage hits that flowing texture, and being able to pipe quickly, evenly and efficiently all takes a lot of time and practice. Each batch is a learning experience. You may have a muggy or rainy day creating havoc in the kitchen. You oven may be far too temperamental. On the other hand, if you're the type of person who counts each stroke of the macaronage stage, your concentration may be tested because someone or something may interrupt you.

CHAPTER 2

Recommended Equipment

You may have some or all of the equipment and ingredients you need in your kitchen. If not, here's a list:

♥ Heavy duty baking sheets/trays

♥ Pastry bag/piping bag and large round tip[s] I like Wilton #10 round tip but you can use a larger one and a different brand.

♥ Parchment paper OR silicone mat[s]

♥ Silicone spatula

♥ Large mesh sieve [strainer] [6" or 8"]

♥ Stainless steel mixing bowls for the meringue; glass or plastic for fillings.

♥ Stand or hand mixer with whipping attachment

♥ Food processer [optional]

♥ Measuring spoons

♥ Cooling rack

♥ Oven thermometer [pictured below]

♥ Digital scale [pictured below]

♥ Covered storage containers/storage bags

♥ Wax paper

♥ Paper macaron template

Digital scale that measures in grams and ounces. An oven thermometer is important for making sure the temperature is accurate.

CHAPTER 3

Macaron Shell Ingredients

Another advantage to baking your own macarons is that you have control over the quality of your ingredients. You can choose organically grown ingredients, eggs from hens that are ethically treated, organic almond flour or opt for pistachio flour or another nut/gluten-free type of flour. Love blackberry buttercream macarons but don't want to drive across town or order them online? Now you can make your own. And yes, I have included a recipe for blackberry buttercream macarons.

The recipes and directions are for the room temperature meringue method known as French meringue. Unlike the Italian meringue method that requires you to boil sugar water, that means there's one less pot to clean and you don't need a candy thermometer.

Here is a list of ingredients to make your wonderful French macarons!

Macaron Shell Ingredients

♥ **Finely ground** almond flour. First of all, almond flour and almond meal is the same thing. If you have access to buying almonds in bulk, stock up. Blanched almonds are recommended if you're looking for a very smooth shell, and they'll have to be **very finely ground** up in a food processor. Notice how I'm stressing that it needs to be finely ground. I've used both Bob's Red Mill and King Arthur brands. Trader Joe's also sells it, but it's from unskinned almonds, not blanched. Of course, there are many available brands. The price is around $12 per pound, which explains why macarons cost about $2.50 each. No matter what kind of almond flour you buy, you still have to sift it at least three more times! Unsifted or minimally sifted almond flour will make your macarons look lumpy.

While almond flour is the most commonly used nut flour, just about any finely ground nut flour can be used. I'm including a recipe that contains part pistachio flour, although macarons can be made with all pistachio flour.

♥ Confectioners' sugar [powdered sugar or icing sugar]. In Australia and the UK, it's easier to find pure icing sugar, which is very finely powdered granulated white sugar. In America, most brands are labeled 10X and contain 3% cornstarch. If allergic to corn, you can find this type of sugar mixed with a small amount of tapioca starch. The 10X does NOT mean it's been sifted ten times, it's the size of the mesh screens that are used to separate powered sugar into three different sizes: 4X, 10X and 14X. 14X is considered the finest, but 10X is the most commonly found in stores.

♥ Granulated sugar -- extra fine, super fine, ultra fine OR caster sugar is recommended. I've made macarons with standard granulated [table] sugar. However, the extra fine is a little nicer as it helps get that smooth shell.

♥ Aged room temperature egg whites. Aged means that they've been out of the shell for several hours, days or even a week [or two]. I haven't noticed much difference although there are macaron bakers who are convinced that the longer an egg white ages, the more moisture has evaporated. It's also supposed to increase the elasticity of the whites, thus helping to prevent runniness, which might ruin your macarons. My best results have been from eggs that have aged for about 14-18 hours. I also prefer using eggs that come from chickens not cooped up in tiny cages. While 'free roaming' eggs cost more, they taste better.

♥ Regular table salt or extra fine salt. It's added midway through the meringue mixing as it helps stabilize the meringue.

♥ Cream of tartar. Serves the same function as salt. Some bakers use half salt and half cream of tartar.

♥ Colorant[s]. I've used three types of colorants: powdered, powdered made with natural ingredients, and gel colorants. Gel colorants are also excellent for brightening the color of your buttercream filling.

♥ Extracts/flavor emulsions/essential oils. I currently don't use any of these as I like to keep the shells as is and let the filling contribute all the flavor. What is the difference between them? Extracts consist of alcohol and the intended flavor. For example, lemon extract contains 90% alcohol, oil of lemon and a tiny bit of water. Remember, alcohol burns off during baking so you won't get that flavor but the aroma and taste of the lemon remain strong.

While I haven't personally used flavor emulsions, they are thick liquids that won't change the consistency of your macaron batter. Oftentimes, they contain flavor and coloring, for example, LorAnn's Red Velvet is obviously red and has a chocolaty/citrusy aroma and taste from what I've read.

Essential oils can be used in the shells but only a few drops are needed. The essential oil must be pure, therapeutic grade and contain NO other additives, like olive or grapeseed oil, to be effective.

Macaron Filling Ingredients

Watching more than 100 videos in my quest to learn how to make macarons, I stumbled across one for making a simple buttercream filling. No butter was used, only shortening. For cream, water was substituted. Therefore, the technical term is actually shortening water. How'd you like that in your macaron or atop a cake or cupcake? Well, in many cases, that's what you get. It does contain one of the other main ingredients, namely powdered sugar a/k/a icing sugar. I understand that this helps prolong the shelf life of the frosting or filling. The only recipes you'll find in *Baking French Macarons: A Beginner's Guide* are ones for a true buttercream filling. And the better the butter, the better the filling!

♥ High quality butter [President, Kerrygold, Plugra or any fresh high fat non-GMO local butter]. Unsalted butter is recommended. Also, the butter should be at room temperature when you're making the filling.

♥ High quality vanilla extract OR vanilla bean paste. Yes, it costs more but the flavor is worth it. Imitation vanilla extract isn't nearly as good. I finally tried vanilla bean paste and recommend it. I use the Neilsen-Massey vanilla bean paste and provide a link for it in **CHAPTER 10: Resources**. I was also curious to try the paste as I'd read several online reviews from bakers of all levels of expertise citing it was very flavorful. According to the website: "Due to its thick consistency, similar to molasses, this culinary paste enables you to add more delicious vanilla flavor without thinning out your batters or sauces. It's also ideal for recipes, such as crème brûlée and ice cream, in which you want to add the enticing visual flair of vanilla seeds." As macaron batter can be finicky, I didn't want to take a chance in adding vanilla extract and I also wanted the vanilla seeds. Win win!

♥ For a rich, flavorful buttercream, use organic cream or heavy cream. High fat creams always taste better! You won't need to use a lot.

♥ Jam filling. Use either a natural jam/fruit spread or fresh fruit. Making a filling with fresh fruit is slightly more labor intensive, but the taste is a lot better. Easy to make recipes for different types of jam are included in CHAPTER 8 – Macaron Filling Recipes.

♥ Extracts/flavor emulsions/essential oils. I used a coconut extract for my buttercream and it was a very good flavor. Not excellent, but I'd make it again as it seemed to be a nice interpretation of coconut.

I prefer using essential oils as I already have several for my soapmaking. I'm very comfortable working with essential oils. Orange, peppermint, and lemon were all used successfully in these recipes. Peppermint is awesome when added to chocolate. Many other essential oils can be used to enhance chocolate and/or buttercreams: lime and just about any citrus essential oil. You can use lavender, rose, allspice [pimento], ginger, spearmint, cornmint, sage or even cinnamon bark -- but go easy! Pure essential oils are very potent, so you'll only need a drop or two for your batch. Always start with just one drop and taste before adding more. Make sure you buy a genuine food-grade essential oil that is NOT diluted with grapeseed or olive oil.

CHAPTER 4

Helpful Tips

♥ Triple sift/sieve almond flour and store in an airtight container. Label and date it if storing for more than a week.

♥ Each time you sift your almond flour, you'll have small pieces left. Save them and use them to put in your breakfast cereal or oatmeal. Alternatively, you can use them as a skin exfoliator, so save it in a small container until you have enough.

♥ Make or find a template online so you have a piping guide [unnecessary if using *marked* silicone mats]. I've included a free template link in **Chapter 11: Recommended Books, Websites & Videos**.

♥ Separate cold eggs and store the egg whites in a cloth or paper towel covered bowl for at least 12 hours. If aging longer, cover with cling wrap and cut a small slit on top. When making macarons, always use ROOM TEMPERATURE egg whites! Make sure you have no bits of yolk or eggshells in the whites. Even a tiny amount of yolk will damage the batter, so if you're breaking them and a bit of yolk falls into the whites, you'll need to start over. Although the below picture of the whites has a yellowish tinge, this is natural, but there aren't any bits of yolk in there. Need help with how to effectively, and quickly, separate eggs? Here are four ways to do it: http://www.wikihow.com/Separate-an-Egg

♥ For your meringue, I recommend a stainless steel mixing bowl. Copper is the best, but don't rush out and spend $100 on one!

Four main meringue ingredients: egg whites, granulated sugar, salt mixed with cream of tartar

♥ Once your meringue is ready, add the flour/sugar mixture right away. Meringue isn't something that you can let sit around as it deflates quickly.

♥ Your utensils and bowls must be CLEAN! Wash and dry them thoroughly before using. Any water or dirt in your mixing bowl or on any utensils might cause your macaron shells to crack or not develop feet. I recommend using white vinegar or fresh lemons and baking soda.

♥ When sifting/sieving the almond flour and confectioners' sugar together, sifting the confectioners' sugar first followed by the almond flour makes it easier to whisk the two ingredients together as the almond flour is heavier.

♥ When mixing the meringue, all of it must be incorporated [this is very evident when coloring your mixture]. When it's almost fully mixed, add the rest of the flour/sugar mixture. The reason for this is that any unmixed meringue may cause cracks in your shells.

♥ Use a tall plastic cup or glass to hold your piping bag. For the macaron filling, add your round tip to the bag, twist the bag to avoid any leakage, and place inside the cup so the tip is facing up. Put the ends of the bag over the glass so it forms a cuff. [I have links at the back of the book for recommended tip sizes.]

♥ Scrape the batter into the piping bag. After it's filled, lay the bag lengthwise on top of a paper towel and push the batter down so there aren't any air pockets. Do this gently but firmly, using a ruler or the edge of a book. Then twist the top and you might want to put a rubber band on it so the batter doesn't ooze out the top.

♥ Hold with your dominant hand and with your other hand direct the tip vertically. Count to three as you're piping each macaron cookie. Then lift up quickly and do the next. You DON'T want little peaks to form on the top because that usually means your batter's undermixed. However, if it's just right, the peak will flatten, especially after you tap the tray on the counter.

♥ If you're right handed, start piping the shells on the left side of the mat, reverse if you're left handed.

♥ Cookie sheets should be doubled to avoid your delicate macaron shells from browning.

♥ After piping your macarons, always bang the cookie sheets on the counter at least 9 or 10 times. You can fold a towel and place it on the counter to help make this part a little quieter.

♥ Let the macarons dry for at least 30 minutes. If possible, set up a floor or table fan nearby to help speed up the drying process. You'll know they're done when you touch the side of one and none of the batter clings to your finger.

♥ Test your oven temperature with an oven thermometer. For my first dozen batches, I was using an oven that ran at least 30 degrees below the necessary temperature. Most home ovens aren't calibrated, so that's why a thermometer is a must-have when baking macarons. General oven temperatures vary but many macaron shells are baked at the 300-degree range [150 Celsius]. Also, make sure your oven's at the right temperature when the preheat beeper sounds. Mine used to be at 180 degrees when that happened!

♥ Note where your heating element is: above or below. If you have problems with macarons being too brown, put an empty cookie sheet on the oven rack directly above the macarons if the heating element is on top. Conversely, if it's below, put the empty baking sheet below them.

♥ Use a reliable digital scale that measures in ounces and grams. They cost about $20 or more but it's well worth it if you plan to make lots of batches of macarons.

♥ A silicone spatula is recommended. You'll need one that is thin and flexible. The head should be plain and not have a hook on one side. This is an essential piece of equipment because it's only used for the macaronage process, the blending of your batter.

♥ When making buttercream filling, SIFT in your powdered sugar so it yields a smoother filling. Oftentimes, powdered sugar will contain lumps due to age and/or humidity.

♥ Jam and jelly fillings will seep through macaron shells faster than buttercream or heavier fillings like peanut butter and Nutella. Therefore, make a smaller batch or be prepared to eat your macarons quickly!

♥ Ideally, the macaron shells will be easy to remove from the silpat or your parchment paper. When that happens, it's a wonderful feeling. After making a couple of batches and having them stick, I went to YouTube to watch yet another how to make macarons video. The person's macarons were picked off the silpat with such ease that I thought it was a trick. Maybe they were stunt macarons or something. When macarons are made correctly, they will be easy to remove. However, if they stick, please don't get frustrated and try to wrestle them off the surface. In some cases, returning them to the oven for a minute or two may help. Then again, it may not. Use a sharp knife or small spatula to pry them off. I've not had any luck in the steaming method of pouring hot water beneath the baking sheet, but you might. Sometimes I throw them away, especially if they come off in bits and chunks. The birds enjoy eating them. However, all isn't lost when that happens. You can crumble them up and sprinkle them on top of your favorite ice cream.

♥ Don't fill your macaron shells until they've cooled off as you don't want your filling to melt. Especially if it's chocolate. Also, make sure you let your macaron shells cool off for at least 10 minutes before removing them from the parchment paper or silpat.

♥ Oatmeal raisin cookies taste great as soon as they come out of the oven. Most cookies do. Macarons don't as they're a bit hard and crispy. Not only should they be served at room temperature, they should also be served about 24 hours later. Have one or two fresh from being filled, but I guarantee you that if you wait, you'll love them even more. The flavors will meld together and the shell will be a little softer and chewier but the outside will still have that nice crunchy texture.

♥ If you've never made macarons before, it's not advisable to make them when it's super hot, the humidity's high and/or it's raining. Macarons despise moisture. Unless you have a kitchen with double pane glass windows, a northern exposure, and everything's well sealed, I don't recommend trying it.

♥ If you don't use all your filling, you can place your piping bag inside a heavy duty Ziploc bag and freeze it for up to 3 months. Make sure you label it and write in the date that it was made.

♥ Take notes when you're making your macarons. I print out each recipe and make notes on the back of it. I calculate the time I start, how long each process takes, how many shells I pipe, how many turn out correctly, how many don't, and how many minutes each batch bakes. I do periodic oven spot checks and note the temperature.

♥ If possible, keep pets away from the baking area. Unfortunately, I can't as there is one cat that prefers hanging out in the kitchen, no matter what the temperature. He once jumped up on the counter, which had three baking sheets with very clean silpat mats awaiting the macaron shells. Apparently, he thought they were a lot of fun to walk across. Thanks to him, I had to wash and dry the mats due to dirty little feet on the silpat, which is unsanitary. Any dirt and oil from the bottom of cat feet could ruin the macarons.

♥ Don't have extra fine granulated sugar/caster sugar? You can run regular granulated sugar through a food processor and in less than a minute, you'll have extra fine sugar!

♥ Cleaning silicone mats isn't difficult if you use very hot water and baking soda and fresh lemon or vinegar.

♥ Bake only one tray of macarons at a time. This isn't time or energy-efficient, but it helps bake the macarons evenly and you can determine if there are any trouble areas this way.

Three Basic Stages in Pictures

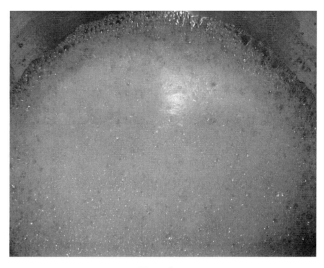

Frothy

~1~ Frothy

When making your meringue, the first stage to watch for is the frothy stage. That's when you add the cream of tartar or salt and part of your granulated sugar. You'll also increase the speed of your mixer. You can add part of your sugar at this stage, or you can wait until the next stage: soft peaks.

North Star

~2~ North Star

This is my nickname for the stage when the meringue is completely mixed and ready. Also known as stiff peak. This is easy to test, as the egg whites will clump to the bottom of the whisk attachment [if using one]. When you remove the whisk attachment, flip it over and see how the egg white points straight north. Also, note how glossy the meringue is.

Ribbons

~3~ Ribbons

The ribbons you'll be looking for are those in the macaronage process that indicate the meringue and the almond flour/sugar mix is ready to be poured into the piping bag. After incorporating the ingredients, lift the spatula above the mixing bowl and watch how the mixture flows in such a way as to create ribbons of batter.

Know Your Oven!

Ever since I dove into baking macarons, I've had problems with my oven. This is why I always use an oven thermometer. My oven may clearly read 300 degrees Fahrenheit but when I look at the oven thermometer, I see that it's 320. Then it'll read 275 a few minutes later. I used to have an oven that was too cold – I'd set it at 320 and the temperature wouldn't budge past 300.

So, no matter if you have a gas, electric, convection or toaster oven, always, always get an oven thermometer and test your temperature. Where are the hot spots? Once you bake a batch of macarons, note if any are browner or darker than others. Then see where that corresponds to in your oven. Know about the all-important heating element – is it on the top, the bottom or located on the top and bottom. Calibrate it if you can. Consult your owner's manual or Google the brand name and model number and find out more about adjusting the temperature.

Here are some handy tips:

♥ Test your oven temperature with an oven thermometer. Most home ovens aren't calibrated, so that's why a thermometer is a must-have when baking macarons. General oven temperatures vary but many macaron shells are baked at the 300-degree range [150 Celsius]. Also, make sure your oven's at the right temperature when the preheat beeper sounds. Mine used to be at 180 degrees when that happened!

♥ Note where your heating element is: above or below. If you have problems with macarons being too brown, put an empty cookie sheet on the oven rack directly above the macarons if the heating element is on top. Conversely, if it's below, put the empty baking sheet below them.

♥ All ovens vary. Some have hot spots, which mean you should be aware of them so you can set your cookie sheets accordingly. Some are very well heated throughout. The instructions for convection ovens vary slightly and you can't put your trays directly in front of the fan.

NOTE: Yes, you can use a toaster oven as long as it's 1500 watts.

CHAPTER 5

Coloring Macaron Shells

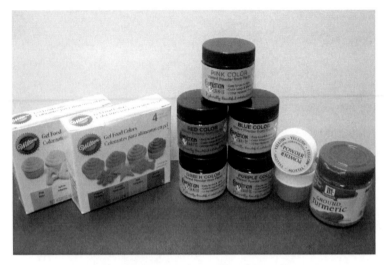

Gel and powdered colorants

One way to make your macarons look enticing is to color them. The color can also be representative of the flavor. For example, blueberry will be blue, lemon will be yellow, green tea will be, you guessed it, green, etc. As macaron shells are so sensitive to liquids being added, standard food coloring isn't recommended as it contains water. Yes, I've seen videos where bakers add several drops of the type of food coloring you find in your grocery store baking aisle, and they turn out fine. But I never felt comfortable risking a batch by adding liquid coloring. Although I tried to avoid that mistake, I still made it with adding too much gel colorant and got green and brown shells rather than the lime green color I was seeking. I didn't think it was possible, but the browned shells were the biggest clue that I'd been trying too hard to get green shells.

Since I also craft soap, I had lots of mica colorants in my soap closet. However, the shimmery purple mica colorant designed for soap didn't work in macaron shells – certainly nothing shimmered and the color turned out more gray than purple.

I've discovered that some powdered additives/natural colorants like cocoa powder and Matcha green tea powder, make the batter a bit heavier and harder to mix. The first time I made chocolate macarons I added more cocoa powder than necessary and I worked up quite a sweat mixing it into the meringue. Even if these natural additives are sifted, they'll still affect the macaronage process so be careful not to add too much.

I've learned an effective way to color macaron shells is by adding the powdered colorant to the almond/sugar mixture rather than the meringue. However, if using a gel colorant, it's best to add that to the meringue. Powder mixes better with dry ingredients, gel mixes better with wet ones.

I bought five small jars of Confection Crafts colorant. They contain natural ingredients. The blue has cabbage leaf and tapioca starch. Purple comes from grape juice and is blended with dextrose. All colors are very fine and don't need to be sifted. These powdered colorants can be added to the meringue just before reaching stiff peak, or to the dry ingredients. I've tried both methods and they work equally well. Several companies in America and other countries make powdered food colorants. Two of the larger ones are Lorann and Americolor. I've tested the yellow and orange Lorann powdered colors and find they color the shells very well.

Whatever brand or type of colorant you choose, always check that brand's recommended measurements as some colorants require a tiny amount while others require more. If in doubt, start with a tiny amount and add more, if necessary.

The shells and fillings pictured here are the results of the various colorants I used. In the recipes, I give the amounts in either drops or teaspoons. Your results will differ if you use a different brand or type of colorant, or if you prefer a darker or lighter shade.

CHAPTER 6

Piping Tips

Even if you've never held a piping /pastry/icing bag before, you can still pipe nice round and similar-sized macaron shells.

If possible, use a round tip. The best size for the Wilton brand ranges from 7 to 12. I've recently discovered that the #10 size works best for me. You may have better luck with a smaller or larger size. Practice and then when you find that right size, make sure you have an extra one as a backup. Ateco is another brand and they can be ordered online or purchased at such stores as Williams-Sonoma, Sur la Table or Bed, Bath & Beyond.

Another alternative is to use just a piping bag and cut the edge off the bottom and don't use a tip at all. This can work just as well.

Maybe you plan to make macarons just once. If so, don't invest in piping bags and/or tips; just use a gallon size Ziploc bag. All you do is cut a quarter-inch size on a bottom corner and there's your homemade piping bag.

Most plastic disposable piping bags are 12" in length, which is suitable for both the macarons, and for any filling you make. Bags are usually sold in packs of 10, 12 or 100.

The easiest way to fill your piping bag is to add the tip and then cut off the bottom part of the bag. Generally, this will be about 1/4" or so. You're ready to place it in a tall cup or glass to fill, but you don't want the batter pouring out of the pastry bag just yet. Twist near the bottom to prevent any mixture from escaping, then place into the cup with the tip facing upwards. The bag should be taller than the cup. You can form a cuff over the rim so it's easy to add the batter.

After you spoon in the batter, it's time to release any excess air and close the top with a rubberband or an icing /piping bag tie.

Filling a piping bag

https://www.youtube.com/watch?v=-X7i1QKAvuA

Piping macarons demonstration

https://www.youtube.com/watch?v=EGiO-UzmL1c

The piping part can still be challenging for me. I always have to remember to squeeze from the top and let gravity help me out!

CHAPTER 7

Macaron Shell Recipes

Basic Macaron Shells

Basic macaron shells with American measurements. This was the first recipe I used. The directions are VERY detailed!

Ingredients:

3/4 cup finely ground almond flour [sift 3 times]

2/3 cup powdered sugar [confectioners' sugar or icing sugar]

2 large egg whites [room temperature]

3 1/2 Tablespoons granulated sugar [caster sugar]

Pinch of cream of tartar or salt

A few drops of your favorite gel color

Oven temperature: 300 degrees Fahrenheit/150 Celsius

Directions:

♥ Stack 2 cookie sheets together. Either download a template or make your own by drawing 1.5" [4 cm] circles that are 1" [2.5 cm] apart. Cover the top cookie sheet with either parchment paper or a silicone mat [silpat] and place over the template.

♥ Sift the almond flour and powdered sugar in a medium bowl. Whisk the ingredients together.

♥ In a very clean and dry [water drops may cause cracks in the macarons] stainless steel or glass bowl, whisk the egg whites. Start at a low setting.

♥ When the whites become frothy like a bubble bath, increase speed to medium. Add the cream of tartar or salt. Continue whisking until there are soft peaks. Add the granulated sugar in 2 or 3 parts.

♥ If using a stand mixer: Increase speed to medium-high, beating until the eggs are glossy and come to a stiff peak. Add gel food coloring. The egg whites will clump at the bottom of the whisk attachment and are stiff. Double check by lifting the whisk attachment up to see if there's a peak that's pointing due north.

♥ If using a hand mixer that contains a whisk attachment: The egg whites will also form a clump at the bottom of the whisk. Double check by lifting the whisk attachment up to see if there's a peak that's pointing due north. Whether using a hand or stand mixer, another test is to pick up your bowl and turn it upside down--nothing should fall or slide out.

♥ Add half of the almond flour mixture to the meringue. Use the silicone spatula to fold the dry ingredients into the meringue. The standard method of mixing is to push down the side of the bowl and fold the mixture over. Fold, fold, fold! Rotate the bowl slightly with each stroke. Generally, the almond flour and sugars will become fairly well mixed at around 20-25 strokes. At first, it'll seem thick and heavy but the flour, sugar and meringue will incorporate. Then, add the rest of the almond flour/sugar blend. The batter will become easier to mix and will look shiny. If using a powdered colorant, once the color is fully blended is usually when the batter is ready. However, you always want to test it by lifting up the spatula and letting a ribbon of batter fall back into the bowl. Using a knife or a wooden craft stick, scrape off the top and base of the spatula to remove all the batter and mix once more to be certain it's well-blended. Also, make sure there are no bits of uncolored/unmixed white meringue along the edges as that will cause cracks in the shells. Run the spatula around the edge of the bowl to make sure it's all incorporated.

♥ Another way to test the batter readiness is when you're able to write the number 8 with the batter.

♥ The macaronage process is the most daunting to bakers of all skill levels as an undermixed batter will result in macarons with no feet and an overmixed batter won't work either as the shells won't rise. The piped macaron batter will end up looking like puddles.

♥ I've read countless recipes where people describe macaron batter as flowing like molten lava. Don't know what that looks like? Here's a link:

https://www.youtube.com/watch?v=ahZD95l1MvM

♥ Scrape batter into a piping bag fitted with a large round tip. After it's filled, place the bag on top of a paper towel and push the batter down so there aren't any air pockets. Do this gently but firmly, using a ruler or the edge of a book. Then twist the top and you might want to put a rubber band on it so the batter doesn't ooze out the top.

♥ A good size macaron shell is 1.5" [4 cm]. Many templates will have discs that size.

♥ Hold piping bag with your dominant hand and with your other hand direct the tip vertically. It's best to count to 3 as you're piping each macaron cookie. Hold the bag about an inch from the center of the circle. Then lift it up quickly and do the next. You DON'T want little peaks to form on the top because that usually means your batter's undermixed. However, if it's just right, the peak will flatten, especially after you tap the tray on the counter.

♥ Remove the template when you're done piping.

♥ This step is very important and it's very easy to do – tap the tray on the countertop several times. You can rotate the tray and repeat the process. Hold the tray firmly by the edges of the parchment paper or silpat so nothing slips. You can place a folded towel on the counter to decrease the noise. Tapping the tray removes any air bubbles from your freshly piped shells. Sometimes you'll see the bubbles disappear, other times you can pop them with a toothpick. Incredibly, some cookbooks and blogs omit this step. When you don't tap the tray on the counter your macarons will crack and look lopsided. The minute or two it takes to tap the tray is worth it!

♥ Let the trays rest in a cool, dry place in your kitchen or in another room if necessary. This is done to dry the batter so that when you touch an edge none of the batter sticks to your finger. When testing, always lightly press your finger against the side so as not to create a dent.

♥ Preheat oven to 300 degrees Fahrenheit/150 Celsius.

♥ You should only bake one tray at a time. Use the center rack or the rack just below it if the oven's heating element is on the top. Reverse this if the heating element is on the bottom—then you'll want your tray to be at the middle rack or one higher.

♥ Check your oven thermometer. If your oven isn't calibrated, you may have to readjust your temperature.

♥ While you're waiting for the shells to dry, you can make your filling.

♥ Bake each tray for about 20 minutes, rotating the pan halfway through baking. The tops should be firm and glossy and the bottoms of the shells should have formed those distinctive "feet" or frills at the bottom. Generally, you'll see feet forming around the 5 to 6-minute mark.

♥ At around 18 minutes, test a macaron to see if it slides off by sliding a spatula beneath one of the macarons. When done, the cookies should lift or slide easily from the parchment or silpat.

♥ Remove from oven and gently slide the parchment or silpat onto a cooling rack. The shells should be cool enough to remove after 10 minutes.

♥ Place macaron shells on a wax paper covered baking sheet or tray for filling. Match the closest sized shells together. For filling your macarons, use a piping bag and the tip size/style is your choice. A star tip can create a nice swirled edge. The plain round tip can be a small to large size. Don't overfill the shells.

Pink Lemonade Macaron Shells

This is another variation of the recipe using American measurements. This recipe uses more sugar.

Pink Lemonade Macaron Shells

Ingredients:

1 cup powdered sugar [confectioners' sugar or icing sugar]

¾ cup almond flour [sift 3 times]

4 Tablespoons granulated sugar

2 egg whites [room temperature]

2 drops pink gel colorant

Pinch of cream of tartar or salt

Oven temperature: 300 degrees Fahrenheit / 150 Celsius

Directions:

♥ Stack 2 cookie sheets together. Either download a template or make your own by drawing 1.5" [4 cm] circles that are 1" [2.5 cm] apart. Cover the top cookie sheet with either parchment paper or a silicone mat [silpat] and place over the template.

♥ Sift the almond flour and powdered sugar in a medium bowl. Whisk the ingredients together.

♥ In a very clean and dry [water drops may cause cracks in the macarons] stainless steel or glass bowl, whisk the egg whites. Start at a low setting.

♥ When the whites become frothy like a bubble bath, increase speed to medium. Add the cream of tartar or salt. Continue whisking until there are soft peaks. Add the granulated sugar in two parts.

♥ If using a stand mixer: Increase speed to medium-high, beating until the eggs are glossy and come to a stiff peak. Add gel food coloring. The egg whites will clump at the bottom of the whisk attachment and are stiff. Double check by lifting the whisk attachment up to see if there's a peak that's pointing due north.

♥ If using a hand mixer that contains a whisk attachment: The egg whites will also form a clump at the bottom of the whisk. Double check by lifting the whisk attachment up to see if there's a peak that's pointing due north. Whether using a hand or stand mixer, another test is to pick up your bowl and turn it upside down--nothing should fall or slide out.

♥ Add half of the almond flour mixture to the meringue. Use the silicone spatula to fold the dry ingredients into the meringue. The standard method of mixing is to push down the side of the bowl and fold the mixture over. Fold, fold, fold! Rotate the bowl slightly with each stroke. Generally, the almond flour and sugars will become fairly well mixed at around 20-25 strokes. At first, it'll seem thick and heavy but the flour, sugar and eggs will incorporate. Then, add the rest of the almond flour/sugar blend. The batter will become easier to mix and will look shiny. If using a powdered colorant, once the color is fully blended is usually when the batter is ready. However, you always want to test it by lifting up the spatula a few inches above the bowl and letting a ribbon of batter fall back into the bowl. Using a knife or a wooden craft stick, scrape off the top and base of the spatula to remove all the batter and mix once more to be certain it's well-blended. Also, make sure there are no bits of uncolored/unmixed white meringue along the edges as that will cause cracks in the shells. Run the spatula around the edge of the bowl to make sure it's all incorporated.

♥ Another way to test the batter readiness is when you're able to write the number 8 with the batter.

♥ The macaronage process is the most daunting to bakers of all skill levels as an undermixed batter will result in macarons with no feet and an overmixed batter won't work either as the shells won't rise. The piped macaron batter will end up looking like puddles.

♥ I've read countless recipes where people describe macaron batter as flowing like molten lava. Don't know what that looks like? Here's a link:

https://www.youtube.com/watch?v=ahZD9511MvM

♥ Scrape batter into a piping bag fitted with a large round tip. After it's filled, place the bag on top of a paper towel and push the batter down so there aren't any air pockets. Do this gently but firmly, using a ruler or the edge of a book. Then twist the top and you might want to put a rubber band on it so the batter doesn't ooze out the top.

♥ A good size macaron shell is 1.5" [4 cm]. Many templates will have discs that size.

♥ Hold piping bag with your dominant hand and with your other hand direct the tip vertically. It's best to count to 3 as you're piping each macaron cookie. Hold the bag about an inch from the center of the circle. Then lift up quickly and do the next. You DON'T want little peaks to form on the top because that usually means your batter's undermixed. However, if it's just right, the peak will flatten, especially after you tap the tray on the counter.

♥ Remove the template when you're done piping.

♥ This step is very important and it's very easy to do – tap the tray on the countertop several times. You can rotate the tray and repeat the process. Hold the tray firmly by the edges of the parchment paper or silpat so nothing slips. You can place a folded towel on the counter to decrease the noise. Tapping the tray removes any air bubbles from your freshly piped shells. Sometimes you'll see the bubbles disappear, other times you can pop them with a toothpick. Incredibly, some cookbooks and blogs omit this step. When you don't tap the tray on the counter your macarons will crack and look lopsided. The minute or two it takes to tap the tray is worth it!

♥ Let the trays rest in a cool, dry place in your kitchen or in another room if necessary. This is done to dry the batter so that when you touch an edge none of the batter sticks to your finger. When testing, always lightly press your finger against the side so as not to create a dent.

♥ Preheat oven to 300 degrees Fahrenheit/150 Celsius.

♥ You should only bake one tray at a time. Use the center rack or the rack just below it if the oven's heating element is on the top. Reverse this if the heating element is on the bottom—then you'll want your tray to be at the middle rack or one higher.

♥ Check your oven thermometer. If your oven isn't calibrated, you may have to readjust your temperature.

♥ While you're waiting for the shells to dry, you can make your filling.

♥ Bake each tray for about 20 minutes, rotating the pan halfway through baking. The tops should be firm and glossy and the bottoms of the shells should have formed those distinctive "feet" or frills at the bottom. Generally, you'll see feet forming around the 5 to 6-minute mark.

♥ At around 18 minutes, test a macaron to see if it slides off by sliding a spatula beneath one of the macarons. When done, the cookies should lift or slide easily from the parchment or silpat.

♥ Remove from oven and gently slide the parchment or silpat onto a cooling rack. The shells should be cool enough to remove after 10 minutes.

♥ Place macaron shells on a wax paper covered baking sheet or tray for filling. Match the closest sized shells together. For filling your macarons, use a piping bag and the tip size/style is your choice. A star tip can create a nice swirled edge. The plain round tip can be a small to large size. Don't overfill the shells.

Lemon Macaron Shells

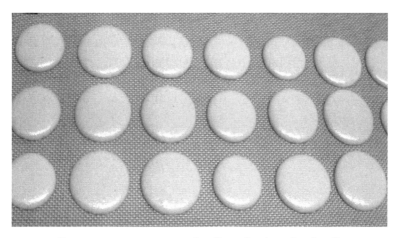

Lemon macarons before being baked

This is my standard recipe. Note that it's in grams.

Ingredients:

100 grams almond flour [sift 3 times]

200 grams powdered sugar

3 large egg whites [room temperature]

50 grams extra fine granulated sugar

Yellow gel food coloring

¼ teaspoon cream of tartar or salt

Oven temperature: 300 degrees Fahrenheit / 150 Celsius

Directions:

♥ Line 3 baking sheets with parchment paper or silpats. Double the baking sheets to prevent browning. Place a template on a baking sheet and put the silpat or parchment paper over it. You can have 3 different templates or just one, which you'll remove after piping each tray. Have a pastry/piping bag with a large round tip ready before you begin.

♥ Sift powdered sugar with the almond flour. Whisk to make sure it's fully blended.

♥ In a stainless steel or glass bowl, beat the egg whites at a low speed until foamy like a bubble bath before adding the cream of tartar. Then add granulated sugar in 3 batches. Increase the speed of your mixer. When finished, the mixture should have stiff peaks. Add color last, but only whip for the briefest amount of time to mix in the color.

♥ Add half the flour/sugar mixture. Fold until the mixture comes together, scraping the sides and flip batter over. The batter will be very thick. When the sugar/flour mixture is blended, the batter will be easier to mix and will look shiny. Lift the spatula and note if the batter falls in ribbons from the spatula. Another test is to "write" the number 8 with the batter.

♥ Scoop batter into piping bag with your spatula. Twist the top of the bag and untwist the bottom, gently pushing the just-poured batter toward the bottom. This removes any excess air.

♥ Pipe batter on the parchment or silpat-lined baking sheets in 1.5-inch circles. Keep the batter just inside circles if using a template.

♥ Rap baking sheet several times on the counter. This will further flatten the macarons, and remove air bubbles. Place a towel on the counter to lessen the noise!

♥ Preheat oven to 300 degrees Fahrenheit / 150 Celsius.

♥ Allow macarons to sit for 30-60 minutes until a film forms. Lightly touch a macaron shell and if no batter clings to your finger then it's dry and ready to be baked.

♥ Bake for approximately 20 minutes. Use either the center rack or the one just below it. After about 10 minutes, rotate the tray. The tops should be firm and glossy and the bottoms of the shells should have formed feet or frills at the bottom. When done, the cookies can easily be removed from the parchment or silpat.

♥ Remove from oven and gently slide the parchment or silpat onto a cooling rack. The shells should be cool enough to remove after 10 minutes.

♥ Place macaron shells on a wax paper covered surface for filling. Match the closest sized shells together. For filling your macarons, use a piping bag and the tip size/style is your choice. Don't overfill the shells.

French Vanilla Bean Macaron Shells

French Vanilla Bean Macaron Shells

Ingredients:

55 grams finely ground almond flour [sift 3 times]

55 grams finely ground pistachio flour [sift 3 times]

200 grams confectioners' sugar

3 large egg whites [room temperature]

1 teaspoon vanilla bean paste [or extract]

50 grams granulated sugar

3 drops blue gel colorant

¼ teaspoon cream of tartar or salt

Oven temperature: 300 Fahrenheit / 150 Celsius

Directions:

♥ Line 3 baking sheets with parchment paper or silpats. Double the baking sheets to prevent browning. Place a template on a baking sheet and put the silpat or parchment paper over it. You can have 3 different templates or just one, which you'll remove after piping each tray. Have a pastry/piping bag with a large round tip ready before you begin.

♥ Sift powdered sugar with the almond flour. Whisk to make sure it's fully blended.

♥ In a stainless steel or glass bowl, beat the egg whites at a low speed until foamy like a bubble bath before adding the cream of tartar. Then add granulated sugar in 3 batches. Increase the speed of your mixer. When finished, the mixture should have stiff peaks. Add color and vanilla bean paste [or extract] last, but only whip for the briefest amount of time to mix in the colors.

♥ Add half the flour/sugar mixture. Fold until the mixture comes together, scraping the sides and flip batter over. The batter will be very thick. When the sugar/flour mixture is blended, the batter will be easier to mix and will look shiny. Lift the spatula and note if the batter falls in ribbons from the spatula. Another test is to "write" the number 8 with the batter.

♥ Scoop batter into piping bag with your spatula. Twist the top of the bag and untwist the bottom, gently pushing the just-poured batter toward the bottom. This removes any excess air.

♥ Pipe batter on the parchment or silpat-lined baking sheets in 1.5-inch circles. Keep the batter just inside circles if using a template.

♥ Rap baking sheet several times on the counter. This will further flatten the macarons, and remove air bubbles. Place a towel on the counter to lessen the noise!

♥ Preheat oven to 300 degrees Fahrenheit / 150 Celsius.

♥ Allow macarons to sit for 30-60 minutes until a film forms. Lightly touch a macaron shell and if no batter clings to your finger then it's dry and ready to be baked.

♥ Bake for approximately 20 minutes. Use either the center rack or the one just below it. After about 10 minutes, rotate the tray. The tops should be firm and glossy and the bottoms of the shells should have formed feet or frills at the bottom. When done, the cookies can easily be removed from the parchment or silpat.

♥ Remove from oven and gently slide the parchment or silpat onto a cooling rack. The shells should be cool enough to remove after 10 minutes.

♥ Place macaron shells on a wax paper covered surface for filling. Match the closest sized shells together. For filling your macarons, use a piping bag and the tip size/style is your choice. Don't overfill the shells.

Double Cherry Macaron Shells

Double Cherry Macaron Shells

Ingredients:

100 grams almond flour [sift 3 times]

200 grams powdered sugar

3 large egg whites at room temperature

50 grams finely granulated sugar

¼ teaspoon cream of tartar or salt

3 drops magenta gel

Oven temperature: 300 Fahrenheit / 150 Celsius

Directions:

♥ Line 3 baking sheets with parchment paper or silpats. Double the baking sheets to prevent browning.

Place a template on a baking sheet and put the silpat or parchment paper over it. You can have 3 different templates or just one, which you'll remove after piping each tray. Have a pastry/piping bag with a large round tip ready before you begin.

♥ Sift powdered sugar with the almond flour. Whisk to make sure it's fully blended.

♥ In a stainless steel or glass bowl, beat the egg whites at a low speed until foamy like a bubble bath before adding the cream of tartar. Then add granulated sugar in 3 batches. Increase the speed of your mixer. When finished, the mixture should have stiff peaks. Add color last, but only whip for the briefest amount of time to mix in the color.

♥ Add half the flour/sugar mixture. Fold until the mixture comes together, scraping the sides and flip batter over. The batter will be very thick. When the sugar/flour mixture is blended, the batter will be easier to mix and will look shiny. Lift the spatula and note if the batter falls in ribbons from the spatula. Another test is to write the number 8 with the batter.

♥ Scoop batter into piping bag with your spatula. Twist the top of the bag and untwist the bottom, gently pushing the just-poured batter toward the bottom. This removes any excess air.

♥ Pipe batter on the parchment or silpat-lined baking sheets in 1.5-inch circles. Keep the batter just inside circles if using a template.

♥ Rap baking sheet several times on the counter. This will further flatten the macarons, and remove air bubbles. Place a towel on the counter to lessen the noise!

♥ Preheat oven to 300 degrees Fahrenheit.

♥ Allow macarons to sit for 30-60 minutes until a film forms. Lightly touch a macaron shell and if no batter clings to your finger then it's dry and ready to be baked.

♥ Bake for approximately 20 minutes. Use either the center rack or the one just below it. After about 10 minutes, rotate the tray. The tops should be firm and glossy and the bottoms of the shells should have formed feet or frills at the bottom. When done, the cookies can easily be removed from the parchment or silpat.

♥ Remove from oven and gently slide the parchment or silpat onto a cooling rack. The shells should be cool enough to remove after 10 minutes.

♥ Place macaron shells on a wax paper covered surface for filling. Match the closest sized shells together. For filling your macarons, use a piping bag and the tip size/style is your choice. Don't overfill the shells.

Peppermint Macaron Shells

Peppermint Macaron Shells

Ingredients:

100 grams almond flour

200 grams powdered sugar

3 large egg whites [room temperature]

50 grams finely granulated sugar

2 teaspoons green powdered colorant [mix into flour/sugar blend]

¼ teaspoon cream of tartar or salt

Oven temperature: 300 degrees Fahrenheit / 150 Celsius

Directions:

♥ Line 3 baking sheets with parchment paper or silpats. Double the baking sheets to prevent browning. Place a template on a baking sheet and put the silpat or parchment paper over it. You can have 3 different templates or just one, which you'll remove after piping each tray. Have a pastry/piping bag with a large round tip ready before you begin.

♥ Sift powdered sugar with the almond flour. Whisk to make sure it's fully blended.

♥ In a stainless steel or glass bowl, beat the egg whites at a low speed until foamy like a bubble bath before adding the cream of tartar. Then add granulated sugar in 3 batches. Increase the speed of your mixer. When finished, the mixture should have stiff peaks.

♥ Add colorant to the flour sugar mixture and then add half the flour/sugar mixture to the meringue. Fold until the mixture comes together, scraping the sides and flip batter over. The batter will be very thick. When the sugar/flour mixture is blended, the batter will be easier to mix and will look shiny. Lift the spatula and note if the batter falls in ribbons from the spatula. Another test is to write the number 8 with the batter.

♥ Scoop batter into piping bag with your spatula. Twist the top of the bag and untwist the bottom, gently pushing the just-poured batter toward the bottom. This removes any excess air.

♥ Pipe batter on the parchment or silpat-lined baking sheets in 1.5-inch circles. Keep the batter just inside circles if using a template.

♥ Rap baking sheet several times on the counter. This will further flatten the macarons, and remove air bubbles. Place a towel on the counter to lessen the noise!

♥ Preheat oven to 300 degrees Fahrenheit.

♥ Allow macarons to sit for 30-60 minutes until a film forms. Lightly touch a macaron shell and if no batter clings to your finger then it's dry and ready to be baked.

♥ Bake for approximately 20 minutes. Use either the center rack or the one just below it. After about 10 minutes, rotate the tray. The tops should be firm and glossy and the bottoms of the shells should have formed feet or frills at the bottom. When done, the cookies can easily be removed from the parchment or silpat.

♥ Remove from oven and gently slide the parchment or silpat onto a cooling rack. The shells should be cool enough to remove after 10 minutes.

♥ Place macaron shells on a wax paper covered surface for filling. Match the closest sized shells together. For filling your macarons, use a piping bag and the tip size/style is your choice. Don't overfill the shells.

Naturally Colored Lemon Macaron Shells

Colored with natural turmeric, you can't taste the spice.

Naturally Colored Lemon Macaron Shells

Ingredients:

100 grams almond flour

200 grams powdered sugar

3 large egg whites [room temperature]

50 grams granulated sugar

1 ¼ teaspoons turmeric [mix into flour/sugar blend]

1/4 teaspoon cream of tartar or salt

Oven temperature: 300 degrees Fahrenheit / 150 Celsius

Directions:

♥ Line 3 baking sheets with parchment paper or silpats. Double the baking sheets to prevent browning. Place a template on a baking sheet and put the silpat or parchment paper over it. You can have 3 different templates or just one, which you'll remove after piping each tray. Have a pastry/piping bag with a large round tip ready before you begin.

♥ Sift powdered sugar with the almond flour. Whisk to make sure it's fully blended.

♥ In a stainless steel or glass bowl, beat the egg whites at a low speed until foamy like a bubble bath before adding the cream of tartar. Then add granulated sugar in 3 batches. Increase the speed of your mixer. When finished, the mixture should have stiff peaks.

♥ Add turmeric to the flour/sugar mixture and then add half the flour/sugar mixture to the meringue. Fold until the mixture comes together, scraping the sides and flip batter over. The batter will be very thick. When the sugar/flour mixture is blended, the batter will be easier to mix and will look shiny. Lift the spatula and note if the batter falls in ribbons from the spatula. Another test is to write the number 8 with the batter.

♥ Scoop batter into piping bag with your spatula. Twist the top of the bag and untwist the bottom, gently pushing the just-poured batter toward the bottom. This removes any excess air.

♥ Pipe batter on the parchment or silpat-lined baking sheets in 1.5-inch circles. Keep the batter just inside circles if using a template.

♥ Rap baking sheet several times on the counter. This will further flatten the macarons, and remove air bubbles. Place a towel on the counter to lessen the noise!

♥ Preheat oven to 300 degrees Fahrenheit.

♥* Allow macarons to sit for 30-60 minutes until a film forms. Lightly touch a macaron shell and if no batter clings to your finger then it's dry and ready to be baked.

♥ Bake for approximately 20 minutes. Use either the center rack or the one just below it. After about 10 minutes, rotate the tray. The tops should be firm and glossy and the bottoms of the shells should have formed feet or frills at the bottom. When done, the cookies can easily be removed from the parchment or silpat.

♥ Remove from oven and gently slide the parchment or silpat onto a cooling rack. The shells should be cool enough to remove after 10 minutes.

♥ Place macaron shells on a wax paper covered surface for filling. Match the closest sized shells together. For filling your macarons, use a piping bag and the tip size/style is your choice. Don't overfill the shells.

Blackberry Macaron Shells

Blackberry Macaron Shells

Ingredients:

100 grams almond flour [sifted 3 times]

200 grams powdered sugar

3 large egg whites [room temperature]

50 grams finely granulated sugar

¼ teaspoon cream of tartar or salt

2 teaspoons *powdered* purple color [mix into flour/sugar blend]

Oven temperature: 300 degrees Fahrenheit/150 Celsius

Directions:

♥ Line 3 baking sheets with parchment paper or silpats. Double the baking sheets to prevent browning. Place a template on a baking sheet and put the silpat or parchment paper over it. You can have 3 different templates or just one, which you'll remove after piping each tray. Have a pastry/piping bag with a large round tip ready before you begin.

♥ Sift powdered sugar with the almond flour. Whisk to make sure it's fully blended.

♥ In a stainless steel or glass bowl, beat the egg whites at a low speed until foamy like a bubble bath before adding the cream of tartar. Then add granulated sugar

in 3 batches. Increase the speed of your mixer. When finished, the mixture should have stiff peaks.

♥ Add powdered colorant to the flour sugar mixture and then add half the flour/sugar mixture to the meringue. Fold until the mixture comes together, scraping the sides and flip batter over. The batter will be very thick. When the sugar/flour mixture is blended, the batter will be easier to mix and will look shiny. Lift the spatula and note if the batter falls in ribbons from the spatula. Another test is to write the number 8 with the batter.

♥ Scoop batter into piping bag with your spatula. Twist the top of the bag and untwist the bottom, gently pushing the just-poured batter toward the bottom. This removes any excess air.

♥ Pipe batter on the parchment or silpat-lined baking sheets in 1.5-inch circles. Keep the batter just inside circles if using a template.

♥ Rap baking sheet several times on the counter. This will further flatten the macarons, and remove air bubbles. Place a towel on the counter to lessen the noise!

♥ Preheat oven to 300 degrees Fahrenheit.

♥ Allow macarons to sit for 30-60 minutes until a film forms. Lightly touch a macaron shell and if no batter clings to your finger then it's dry and ready to be baked.

♥ Bake for approximately 20 minutes. Use either the center rack or the one just below it. After about 10 minutes, rotate the tray. The tops should be firm and glossy and the bottoms of the shells should have formed feet or frills at the bottom. When done, the cookies can easily be removed from the parchment or silpat.

♥ Remove from oven and gently slide the parchment or silpat onto a cooling rack. The shells should be cool enough to remove after 10 minutes.

♥ Place macaron shells on a wax paper covered surface for filling. Match the closest sized shells together. For filling your macarons, use a piping bag and the tip size/style is your choice. Don't overfill the shells.

Raspberry Macaron Shells

Raspberry Macaron Shells

Ingredients:

100 grams almond flour

200 grams powdered sugar

3 large egg whites [room temperature]

50 grams finely granulated sugar

¼ teaspoon cream of tartar or salt

2 teaspoons *powdered* red color [mix into flour/sugar blend]

Oven temperature: 300 degrees Fahrenheit/150 Celsius

Directions:

♥ Line 3 baking sheets with parchment paper or silpats. Double the baking sheets to prevent browning. Place a template on a baking sheet and put the silpat or parchment paper over it. You can have 3 different templates or just one, which you'll remove after piping each tray. Have a pastry/piping bag with a large round tip ready before you begin.

♥ Sift powdered sugar with the almond flour. Whisk to make sure it's fully blended.

♥ In a stainless steel or glass bowl, beat the egg whites at a low speed until foamy like a bubble bath before adding the cream of tartar. Then add granulated sugar

in 3 batches. Increase the speed of your mixer. When finished, the mixture should have stiff peaks.

♥ Add powdered colorant to the flour sugar mixture and then add half the flour/sugar mixture to the meringue. Fold until the mixture comes together, scraping the sides and flip batter over. The batter will be very thick. When the sugar/flour mixture is blended, the batter will be easier to mix and will look shiny. Lift the spatula and note if the batter falls in ribbons from the spatula. Another test is to write the number 8 with the batter.

♥ Scoop batter into piping bag with your spatula. Twist the top of the bag and untwist the bottom, gently pushing the just-poured batter toward the bottom. This removes any excess air.

♥ Pipe batter on the parchment or silpat-lined baking sheets in 1.5-inch circles. Keep the batter just inside circles if using a template.

♥ Rap baking sheet several times on the counter. This will further flatten the macarons, and remove air bubbles. Place a towel on the counter to lessen the noise!

♥ Preheat oven to 300 degrees Fahrenheit/150 Celsius.

♥ Allow macarons to sit for 30-60 minutes until a film forms. Lightly touch a macaron shell and if no batter clings to your finger then it's dry and ready to be baked.

♥ Bake for approximately 20 minutes. Use either the center rack or the one just below it. After about 10 minutes, rotate the tray. The tops should be firm and glossy and the bottoms of the shells should have formed feet or frills at the bottom. When done, the cookies can easily be removed from the parchment or silpat.

♥ Remove from oven and gently slide the parchment or silpat onto a cooling rack. The shells should be cool enough to remove after 10 minutes.

♥ Place macaron shells on a wax paper covered surface for filling. Match the closest sized shells together. For filling your macarons, use a piping bag and the tip size/style is your choice. Don't overfill the shells.

Blueberry Macaron Shells

Blueberry Macaron Shells

Ingredients:

100 grams almond flour

200 grams powdered sugar

3 large egg whites [room temperature]

50 grams finely granulated sugar

¼ teaspoon cream of tartar or salt

1 teaspoon powdered blue color [mix into flour/sugar blend]

Oven temperature: 300 degrees Fahrenheit/150 Celsius

Directions:

♥ Line 3 baking sheets with parchment paper or silpats. Double the baking sheets to prevent browning.

Place a template on a baking sheet and put the silpat or parchment paper over it. You can have 3 different templates or just one, which you'll remove after piping each tray. Have a pastry/piping bag with a large round tip ready before you begin.

♥ Sift powdered sugar with the almond flour. Whisk to make sure it's fully blended.

♥ In a stainless steel or glass bowl, beat the egg whites at a low speed until foamy like a bubble bath before adding the cream of tartar. Then add granulated sugar in 3 batches. Increase the speed of your mixer. When finished, the mixture should have stiff peaks.

♥ Add powdered colorant to the flour sugar mixture and then add half the flour/sugar mixture to the meringue. Fold until the mixture comes together, scraping the sides and flip batter over. The batter will be very thick. When the sugar/flour mixture is blended, the batter will be easier to mix and will look shiny. Lift the spatula and note if the batter falls in ribbons from the spatula. Another test is to write the number 8 with the batter.

♥ Scoop batter into piping bag with your spatula. Twist the top of the bag and untwist the bottom, gently pushing the just-poured batter toward the bottom. This removes any excess air.

♥ Pipe batter on the parchment or silpat-lined baking sheets in 1.5-inch circles. Keep the batter just inside circles if using a template.

♥ Rap baking sheet several times on the counter. This will further flatten the macarons, and remove air bubbles. Place a towel on the counter to lessen the noise!

♥ Preheat oven to 300 degrees Fahrenheit/150 Celsius.

♥ Allow macarons to sit for 30-60 minutes until a film forms. Lightly touch a macaron shell and if no batter clings to your finger then it's dry and ready to be baked.

♥ Bake for approximately 20 minutes. Use either the center rack or the one just below it. After about 10 minutes, rotate the tray. The tops should be firm and glossy and the bottoms of the shells should have formed feet or frills at the bottom. When done, the cookies can easily be removed from the parchment or silpat.

♥ Remove from oven and gently slide the parchment or silpat onto a cooling rack. The shells should be cool enough to remove after 10 minutes.

♥ Place macaron shells on a wax paper covered surface for filling. Match the closest sized shells together. For filling your macarons, use a piping bag and the tip size/style is your choice. Don't overfill the shells.

Key Lime Macaron Shells

The dark green contrasts nicely with the lightly colored Key lime filling.

Key Lime Macaron Shells

Ingredients:

100 grams almond flour

200 grams powdered sugar

3 large egg whites [room temperature]

50 grams granulated sugar

1.5 teaspoons powdered green colorant [mix into flour/sugar blend]

1/4 teaspoon cream of tartar or salt

Oven Temperature: 300 degrees Fahrenheit/150 Celsius

Directions:

♥ Line 3 baking sheets with parchment paper or silpats. Double the baking sheets to prevent browning. Place a template on a baking sheet and put the silpat or parchment paper over it. You can have 3 different templates or just one, which you'll remove after piping each tray. Have a pastry/piping bag with a large round tip ready before you begin.

♥ Sift powdered sugar with the almond flour. Whisk to make sure it's fully blended.

♥ In a stainless steel or glass bowl, beat the egg whites at a low speed until foamy like a bubble bath before adding the cream of tartar. Then add granulated sugar in 3 batches. Increase the speed of your mixer. When finished, the mixture should have stiff peaks.

♥ Add powdered colorant to the flour sugar mixture and then add half the flour/sugar mixture to the meringue. Fold until the mixture comes together, scraping the sides and flip batter over. The batter will be very thick. When the sugar/flour mixture is blended, the batter will be easier to mix and will look shiny. Lift the spatula and note if the batter falls in ribbons from the spatula. Another test is to write the number 8 with the batter.

♥ Scoop batter into piping bag with your spatula. Twist the top of the bag and untwist the bottom, gently pushing the just-poured batter toward the bottom. This removes any excess air.

♥ Pipe batter on the parchment or silpat-lined baking sheets in 1.5-inch circles. Keep the batter just inside circles if using a template.

♥ Rap baking sheet several times on the counter. This will further flatten the macarons, and remove air bubbles. Place a towel on the counter to lessen the noise!

♥ Preheat oven to 300 degrees Fahrenheit/150 Celsius.

♥ Allow macarons to sit for 30-60 minutes until a film forms. Lightly touch a macaron shell and if no batter clings to your finger then it's dry and ready to be baked.

♥ Bake for approximately 20 minutes. Use either the center rack or the one just below it. After about 10 minutes, rotate the tray. The tops should be firm and glossy and the bottoms of the shells should have formed feet or frills at the bottom. When done, the cookies can easily be removed from the parchment or silpat.

♥ Remove from oven and gently slide the parchment or silpat onto a cooling rack. The shells should be cool enough to remove after 10 minutes.

♥ Place macaron shells on a wax paper covered surface for filling. Match the closest sized shells together. For filling your macarons, use a piping bag and the tip size/style is your choice. Don't overfill the shells.

Tangy Orange Macaron Shells

Tangy Orange Macaron Shells

Ingredients:

100 grams almond flour

200 grams powdered sugar

3 large egg whites [room temperature]

50 grams granulated sugar

½ teaspoon powdered orange colorant

1/8 teaspoon salt

1/8 teaspoon cream of tartar

Oven Temperature: 300 degrees Fahrenheit/150 Celsius

Directions:

♥ Line 3 baking sheets with parchment paper or silpats. Double the baking sheets to prevent browning. Place a template on a baking sheet and put the silpat or parchment paper over it. You can have 3 different templates or just one, which you'll remove after piping each tray. Have a pastry/piping bag with a large round tip ready before you begin.

♥ Sift powdered sugar with the almond flour. Whisk to make sure it's fully blended.

♥ In a stainless steel or glass bowl, beat the egg whites at a low speed until foamy like a bubble bath before adding the cream of tartar. Then add granulated sugar in 3 batches. Increase the speed of your mixer. When finished, the mixture should have stiff peaks.

♥ Add powdered colorant to the flour sugar mixture and then add half the flour/sugar mixture to the meringue. Fold until the mixture comes together, scraping the sides and flip batter over. The batter will be very thick. When the sugar/flour mixture is blended, the batter will be easier to mix and will look shiny. Lift the spatula and note if the batter falls in ribbons from the spatula. Another test is to write the number 8 with the batter.

♥ Scoop batter into piping bag with your spatula. Twist the top of the bag and untwist the bottom, gently pushing the just-poured batter toward the bottom. This removes any excess air.

♥ Pipe batter on the parchment or silpat-lined baking sheets in 1.5-inch circles. Keep the batter just inside circles if using a template.

♥ Rap baking sheet several times on the counter. This will further flatten the macarons, and remove air bubbles. Place a towel on the counter to lessen the noise!

♥ Preheat oven to 300 degrees Fahrenheit/150 Celsius.

♥ Allow macarons to sit for 30-60 minutes until a film forms. Lightly touch a macaron shell and if no batter clings to your finger then it's dry and ready to be baked.

♥ Bake for approximately 20 minutes. Use either the center rack or the one just below it. After about 10 minutes, rotate the tray. The tops should be firm and glossy and the bottoms of the shells should have formed feet or frills at the bottom. When done, the cookies can easily be removed from the parchment or silpat.

♥ Remove from oven and gently slide the parchment or silpat onto a cooling rack. The shells should be cool enough to remove after 10 minutes.

♥ Place macaron shells on a wax paper covered surface for filling. Match the closest sized shells together. For filling your macarons, use a piping bag and the tip size/style is your choice. Don't overfill the shells.

Coconut Macaron Shells

These were going to be lemon coconut but I decided to leave out the lemon at the last minute.

Coconut Macaron Shells

Ingredients:

100 grams almond flour

200 grams powdered sugar

3 large egg whites [room temperature]

50 grams granulated sugar

1/8 teaspoon cream of tartar

1/8 teaspoon salt

1 teaspoon yellow powdered food color

Oven Temperature: 300 Fahrenheit / 150 Celsius

Directions:

♥ Line 3 baking sheets with parchment paper or silpats. Double the baking sheets to prevent browning. Place a template on a baking sheet and put the silpat or parchment paper over it. You can have 3 different templates or just one, which you'll remove after piping each tray. Have a pastry/piping bag with a large round tip ready before you begin.

♥ Sift powdered sugar with the almond flour. Whisk to make sure it's fully blended.

♥ In a stainless steel or glass bowl, beat the egg whites at a low speed until foamy like a bubble bath before adding the cream of tartar. Then add granulated sugar in 3 batches. Increase the speed of your mixer. When finished, the mixture should have stiff peaks.

♥ Add powdered colorant to the flour/sugar mixture and then add half the flour/sugar mixture to the meringue. Fold until the mixture comes together, scraping the sides and flip batter over. The batter will be very thick. When the sugar/flour mixture is blended, the batter will be easier to mix and will look shiny. Lift the spatula and note if the batter falls in ribbons from the spatula. Another test is to write the number 8 with the batter.

♥ Scoop batter into piping bag with your spatula. Twist the top of the bag and untwist the bottom, gently pushing the just-poured batter toward the bottom. This removes any excess air.

♥ Pipe batter on the parchment or silpat-lined baking sheets in 1.5-inch circles. Keep the batter just inside circles if using a template.

♥ Rap baking sheet several times on the counter. This will further flatten the macarons, and remove air bubbles. Place a towel on the counter to lessen the noise!

♥ Preheat oven to 300 degrees Fahrenheit/150 Celsius.

♥ Allow macarons to sit for 30-60 minutes until a film forms. Lightly touch a macaron shell and if no batter clings to your finger then it's dry and ready to be baked.

♥ Bake for approximately 20 minutes. Use either the center rack or the one just below it. After about 10 minutes, rotate the tray. The tops should be firm and glossy and the bottoms of the shells should have formed feet or frills at the bottom. When done, the cookies can easily be removed from the parchment or silpat.

♥ Remove from oven and gently slide the parchment or silpat onto a cooling rack. The shells should be cool enough to remove after 10 minutes.

♥ Place macaron shells on a wax paper covered surface for filling. Match the closest sized shells together. For filling your macarons, use a piping bag and the tip size/style is your choice. Don't overfill the shells.

Orange Chocolate Macaron Shells

Orange Chocolate Macaron Shells

Ingredients:

100 grams almond flour

200 grams powdered sugar

3 large egg whites [room temperature]

50 grams granulated sugar

1/4 teaspoon cream of tartar

½ teaspoon powdered orange food color

Oven Temperature: 300 degrees Fahrenheit/150 Celsius

Directions:

♥ Line 3 baking sheets with parchment paper or silpats. Double the baking sheets to prevent browning. Place a template on a baking sheet and put the silpat or parchment paper over it. You can have 3 different templates or just one, which you'll remove after piping each tray. Have a pastry/piping bag with a large round tip ready before you begin.

♥ Sift powdered sugar with the almond flour. Whisk to make sure it's fully blended.

♥ In a stainless steel or glass bowl, beat the egg whites at a low speed until foamy like a bubblc bath before adding the cream of tartar. Then add granulated sugar

in 3 batches. Increase the speed of your mixer. When finished, the mixture should have stiff peaks.

♥ Add powdered colorant to the flour sugar mixture and then add half the flour/sugar mixture to the meringue. Fold until the mixture comes together, scraping the sides and flip batter over. The batter will be very thick. When the sugar/flour mixture is blended, the batter will be easier to mix and will look shiny. Lift the spatula and note if the batter falls in ribbons from the spatula. Another test is to write the number 8 with the batter.

♥ Scoop batter into piping bag with your spatula. Twist the top of the bag and untwist the bottom, gently pushing the just-poured batter toward the bottom. This removes any excess air.

♥ Pipe batter on the parchment or silpat-lined baking sheets in 1.5-inch circles. Keep the batter just inside circles if using a template.

♥ Rap baking sheet several times on the counter. This will further flatten the macarons, and remove air bubbles. Place a towel on the counter to lessen the noise!

♥ Preheat oven to 300 degrees Fahrenheit/150 Celsius.

♥ Allow macarons to sit for 30-60 minutes until a film forms. Lightly touch a macaron shell and if no batter clings to your finger then it's dry and ready to be baked.

♥ Bake for approximately 20 minutes. Use either the center rack or the one just below it. After about 10 minutes, rotate the tray. The tops should be firm and glossy and the bottoms of the shells should have formed feet or frills at the bottom. When done, the cookies can easily be removed from the parchment or silpat.

♥ Remove from oven and gently slide the parchment or silpat onto a cooling rack. The shells should be cool enough to remove after 10 minutes.

♥ Place macaron shells on a wax paper covered surface for filling. Match the closest sized shells together. For filling your macarons, use a piping bag and the tip size/style is your choice. Don't overfill the shells.

Mint Chocolate Macaron Shells

The cooling, refreshing taste of minty chocolate is guaranteed to please any chocolate lover!

Mint Chocolate Macaron Shells

Ingredients:

100 grams almond flour

200 grams powdered sugar

3 large egg whites

50 grams finely granulated sugar

¼ teaspoon cream of tartar

1/2 teaspoon natural green powdered colorant

Temperature: 300 degrees Fahrenheit/150 Celsius

Directions:

♥ Line 3 baking sheets with parchment paper or silpats. Double the baking sheets to prevent browning.

Place a template on a baking sheet and put the silpat or parchment paper over it. You can have 3 different templates or just one, which you'll remove after piping each tray. Have a pastry/piping bag with a large round tip ready before you begin.

♥ Sift powdered sugar with the almond flour. Whisk to make sure it's fully blended.

♥ In a stainless steel or glass bowl, beat the egg whites at a low speed until foamy like a bubble bath before adding the cream of tartar. Then add granulated sugar in 3 batches. Increase the speed of your mixer. When finished, the mixture should have stiff peaks.

♥ Add powdered colorant to the flour sugar mixture and then add half the flour/sugar mixture to the meringue. Fold until the mixture comes together, scraping the sides and flip batter over. The batter will be very thick. When the sugar/flour mixture is blended, the batter will be easier to mix and will look shiny. Lift the spatula and note if the batter falls in ribbons from the spatula. Another test is to write the number 8 with the batter.

♥ Scoop batter into piping bag with your spatula. Twist the top of the bag and untwist the bottom, gently pushing the just-poured batter toward the bottom. This removes any excess air.

♥ Pipe batter on the parchment or silpat-lined baking sheets in 1.5-inch circles. Keep the batter just inside circles if using a template.

♥ Rap baking sheet several times on the counter. This will further flatten the macarons, and remove air bubbles. Place a towel on the counter to lessen the noise!

♥ Preheat oven to 300 degrees Fahrenheit/150 Celsius.

♥ Allow macarons to sit for 30-60 minutes until a film forms. Lightly touch a macaron shell and if no batter clings to your finger then it's dry and ready to be baked.

♥ Bake for approximately 20 minutes. Use either the center rack or the one just below it. After about 10 minutes, rotate the tray. The tops should be firm and glossy and the bottoms of the shells should have formed feet or frills at the bottom. When done, the cookies can easily be removed from the parchment or silpat.

♥ Remove from oven and gently slide the parchment or silpat onto a cooling rack. The shells should be cool enough to remove after 10 minutes.

♥ Place macaron shells on a wax paper covered surface for filling. Match the closest sized shells together. For filling your macarons, use a piping bag and the tip size/style is your choice. Don't overfill the shells.

Cinnamon Macaron Shells

Uncolored shells sprinkled with finely powdered cinnamon and paired with homemade caramel filling.

Cinnamon Macaron Shells

Ingredients:

100 grams almond flour

200 grams powdered sugar

3 large egg whites

50 grams finely granulated sugar

¼ teaspoon cream of tartar

powdered cinnamon for sprinkling over shells

Temperature: 300 degrees Fahrenheit / 150 Celsius

Directions:

♥ Line 3 baking sheets with parchment paper or silpats. Double the baking sheets to prevent browning. Place a template on a baking sheet and put the silpat or parchment paper over it. You can have 3 different templates or just one, which you'll remove after piping each tray. Have a pastry/piping bag with a large round tip ready before you begin.

♥ Sift powdered sugar with the almond flour. Whisk to make sure it's fully blended.

♥ In a stainless steel or glass bowl, beat the egg whites at a low speed until foamy like a bubble bath before adding the cream of tartar. Then add granulated sugar in 3 batches. Increase the speed of your mixer. When finished, the mixture should have stiff peaks.

♥ Add half the flour/sugar mixture to the meringue. Fold until the mixture comes together, scraping the sides and flip batter over. The batter will be very thick. When the sugar/flour mixture is blended, the batter will be easier to mix and will look shiny. Lift the spatula and note if the batter falls in ribbons from the spatula. Another test is to write the number 8 with the batter.

♥ Scoop batter into piping bag with your spatula. Twist the top of the bag and untwist the bottom, gently pushing the just-poured batter toward the bottom. This removes any excess air.

♥ Pipe batter on the parchment or silpat-lined baking sheets in 1.5-inch circles. Keep the batter just inside circles if using a template.

♥ Rap baking sheet several times on the counter. This will further flatten the macarons, and remove air bubbles. Place a towel on the counter to lessen the noise! Sprinkle cinnamon on top of the shells. For a lighter coating, use a small sieve.

♥ Preheat oven to 300 degrees Fahrenheit/150 Celsius.

♥ Allow macarons to sit for 30-60 minutes until a film forms. Lightly touch a macaron shell and if no batter clings to your finger then it's dry and ready to be baked.

♥ Bake for approximately 20 minutes. Use either the center rack or the one just below it. After about 10 minutes, rotate the tray. The tops should be firm and glossy and the bottoms of the shells should have formed feet or frills at the bottom. When done, the cookies can easily be removed from the parchment or silpat.

♥ Remove from oven and gently slide the parchment or silpat onto a cooling rack. The shells should be cool enough to remove after 10 minutes.

♥ Place macaron shells on a wax paper covered surface for filling. Match the closest sized shells together. For filling your macarons, use a piping bag and the tip size/style is your choice. Don't overfill the shells.

One of the shells undersides that didn't get brown after being baked. Most were slightly brown but a few came out this color!

Acai Macaron Shells

My goal was to make a "healthy" macaron by using acai powder, which is considered an Amazon superfruit. I bought some freeze-dried acai powder at a health food store. I ended up sprinkling the powder on top rather than incorporating the lovely purple powder in the shells. The reason for this is that the texture isn't fine and it's not completely dry. It would have to be dried in the oven for several minutes, and then finely ground in a food processor and sifted to get the right texture. The clumps of acai powder give the macaron shells character, along with a touch of the blueberry-like flavor.

Acai Macaron Shells

Ingredients:

100 grams almond flour

200 grams powdered sugar

3 large egg whites

50 grams finely granulated sugar

¼ teaspoon cream of tartar

¾ teaspoon powdered natural purple colorant

Acai powder for sprinkling over shells

Temperature: 300 degrees Fahrenheit / 150 Celsius

Directions:

♥ Line 3 baking sheets with parchment paper or silpats. Double the baking sheets to prevent browning. Place a template on a baking sheet and put the silpat or parchment paper over it. You can have 3 different templates or just one, which you'll remove after piping each tray. Have a pastry/piping bag with a large round tip ready before you begin.

♥ Sift powdered sugar with the almond flour. Whisk to make sure it's fully blended.

♥ In a stainless steel or glass bowl, beat the egg whites at a low speed until foamy like a bubble bath before adding the cream of tartar. Then add granulated sugar in 3 batches. Increase the speed of your mixer. When finished, the mixture should have stiff peaks.

♥ Add powdered colorant to the flour sugar mixture and then add half the flour/sugar mixture to the meringue. Fold until the mixture comes together, scraping the sides and flip batter over. The batter will be very thick. When the sugar/flour mixture is blended, the batter will be easier to mix and will look shiny. Lift the spatula and note if the batter falls in ribbons from the spatula. Another test is to write the number 8 with the batter.

♥ Scoop batter into piping bag with your spatula. Twist the top of the bag and untwist the bottom, gently pushing the just-poured batter toward the bottom. This removes any excess air.

♥ Pipe batter on the parchment or silpat-lined baking sheets in 1.5-inch circles. Keep the batter just inside circles if using a template.

♥ Rap baking sheet several times on the counter. This will further flatten the macarons, and remove air bubbles. Place a towel on the counter to lessen the noise! Sprinkle acai powder on top of the shells.

♥ Preheat oven to 300 degrees Fahrenheit/150 Celsius.

♥ Allow macarons to sit for 30-60 minutes until a film forms. Lightly touch a macaron shell and if no batter clings to your finger then it's dry and ready to be baked.

♥ Bake for approximately 20 minutes. Use either the center rack or the one just below it. After about 10 minutes, rotate the tray. The tops should be firm and glossy and the bottoms of the shells should have formed feet or frills at the bottom. When done, the cookies can easily be removed from the parchment or silpat.

♥ Remove from oven and gently slide the parchment or silpat onto a cooling rack. The shells should be cool enough to remove after 10 minutes.

♥ Place macaron shells on a wax paper covered surface for filling. Match the closest sized shells together. For filling your macarons, use a piping bag and the tip size/style is your choice. Don't overfill the shells.

CHAPTER 8

Macaron Filling Recipes

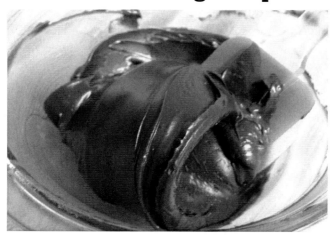

Chocolate ganache filling

The filling is what creates the taste of the macaron. No matter what color your macaron shell is, the white ones will taste the same as the green ones. The only way this changes is if you add extract or a powdered colorant like cocoa powder or powdered fruit to the shells. You can add flavor to your shell, but for some that may be too intense. As noted in all the recipes, the shell formula doesn't vary—egg whites, almond flour, and two types of sugar. The plain shells taste sweet and the texture is crispy.

A note about the buttercream filling recipes: these are technically American buttercream. They don't contain egg yolks or egg whites, so the filling will last a little longer than the types of buttercream made with eggs.

When making buttercream fillings, you should try to use the finest ingredients available like European-style butters or local butters made with at least 82% butterfat. I use high-quality brands like President, Plugra or Kerry Gold.

If you can obtain 85% to 90% butterfat, you'll have the tastiest buttercream fillings ever!

I also recommend sifting the confectioners' sugar before adding it to the butter. Depending on the brand of sugar and your climate, the sugar may have lumps in it. Sifting will automatically eliminate the lumps and you'll get a smoother, fluffier filling.

All recipes are in both American cup measurements and have been converted to grams for those of you who prefer to bake with precision. Measurements for the fillings don't have to be as precise as those for the macaron shells. I haven't converted teaspoons but I have for all measurements one tablespoon and above. I've also rounded the numbers because it's easier to weigh and the amounts won't alter the recipe.

Colorants are listed by drops as I used gel colorants the buttercreams. You can also use regular liquid food coloring.

For buttercream fillings, you can presift your powdered sugar or sift as you're adding it to the butter. Personally, I find the presifting method easier.

Heavy cream is what I used in all the buttercream filling recipes. This is the highest fat cream available in the United States. For those of you in the U.K., clotted cream has 55% fat, and double cream contains 48% fat.

NOTE: If you have extra filling left after filling your macarons, you can put your piping bag in a freezer safe Ziploc bag and freeze for up to 3 months.

Strawberry Buttercream Filling

Strawberry Buttercream Filling

Ingredients:

¼ cup softened butter [60 grams]

1 ½ cups presifted powdered sugar/confectioners' sugar/icing sugar [188 grams]

2 Tablespoons heavy cream [15 grams]

4 Tablespoons strawberry jam [56 grams]

1 teaspoon pure vanilla extract OR vanilla bean paste

Pink colorant [optional]

Directions:

If using a stand mixer, add the butter to the bowl and mix for about 30 seconds, and then add half the powdered sugar.

If using a hand mixer, make sure you have a LARGE bowl and mix the butter first, then add half the sugar.

When the mixture is smooth, add your wet ingredients: cream, jam, vanilla and colorant. Once mixed, add the remaining powdered sugar.

Lemon Curd Buttercream Filling

Lemon Curd Buttercream Filling

Ingredients:

1/4 cup softened butter [60 grams]

1 1/2 cups presifted powdered sugar/confectioners' sugar/icing sugar [188 grams]

2 Tablespoons heavy cream [15 grams]

3 Tablespoons lemon curd [42 grams]

1 teaspoon vanilla extract or vanilla bean paste

5 drops yellow gel color [optional]

Directions:

Whip butter for about 2 minutes before adding some of the powdered sugar. Add the cream, lemon curd and vanilla. Gradually add the remaining powdered sugar until the filling is the desired consistency. Add colorant last.

Lemon Butter Curd Filling

Lemon Butter Curd Filling

Ingredients:

1/4 cup softened butter [60 grams]

1 cup presifted powdered sugar/confectioners' sugar/icing sugar [125 grams]

5 Tablespoons lemon curd [70 grams]

1 teaspoon vanilla bean paste

Yellow gel colorant [optional]

This recipe is for those who adore the tart and tangy taste of lemon. I came up with this recipe when I decided that I wanted more lemon and less sugar. The need for heavy cream is totally unnecessary. The addition of yellow gel colorant brightens the filling.

Directions:

Blend the softened butter with half of the powdered sugar. Add the cream, lemon curd and vanilla. Gradually add the remaining powdered sugar until the filling is the desired consistency.

French Vanilla Buttercream Filling

French Vanilla Buttercream Filling

Ingredients:

1/4 Cup softened butter [60 grams]

1 1/2 Cups presifted powdered sugar/confectioners' sugar/icing sugar [188 grams]

3 Tablespoons heavy cream [22 grams]

2 teaspoons vanilla bean paste

Directions:

Add the butter to a large bowl and mix for about 30 seconds, and then add half the powdered sugar.

When the mixture is smooth, add your wet ingredients: cream and vanilla. Once mixed, it's time to add the remaining powdered sugar.

Blackberry Jam Filling

Blackberry jam with a dollop of blackberry buttercream

Blackberry Jam Filling

Ingredients:

8 ounces fresh blackberries [220 grams]

1 ¾ cups granulated sugar/white sugar [350 grams]

Sliver of unsalted butter

1 1/2 Tablespoons *liquid* pectin

2 8-ounce jars [one is for jam, the other is for the macarons]

Directions:

Mash up the blackberries in a medium sized bowl with a fork or a potato masher.

Strain if you don't want any seeds.

Pour berries into a very large saucepan or pot [6-8 quarts in size]. The fruit will cover the bottom in a thin layer.

Turn the burner to high.

Add the sugar, stirring the ingredients.

Add the sliver of butter to break up foam.

When the mixture reaches a full rolling boil that doesn't stop even when stirred, add the pectin.

Once the pectin has been quickly added, allow to boil for 1 minute.

Turn off heat and remove from burner.

Pour into glass jars. One is for the macarons, the other is for you.

Wait about an hour or until cooled down. Pour into a pastry bag with a large round tip.

Note: pouring directly into a plastic pastry bag would cause it to melt.

Blackberry Buttercream Filling

Blackberry jam and buttercream fillings

Blackberry Buttercream Filling

Ingredients:

4 ounces softened butter [120 grams]

1 ¼ cups presifted powdered sugar/confectioners' sugar/icing sugar [156 grams]

4 ounces fresh blackberries [110 grams]

1 Tablespoon heavy cream

1 teaspoon vanilla bean paste

3 drops purple gel colorant [optional]

Directions:

Beat softened butter on medium speed for about 3-4 minutes until completely smooth and creamy. Add powdered sugar, cream, vanilla extract and blackberries with the mixer running. Increase to high speed and beat until thick and creamy, about 5 full minutes, so it's very soft and fluffy.

Raspberry Jam Filling

Raspberry jam tastes wonderful in macrons. It's one of the most popular flavors.

Raspberry Jam Filling

Ingredients:

8 ounces fresh raspberries [220 grams]

1 ¾ cups granulated sugar/white sugar [350 grams]

Sliver unsalted butter

1 1/2 Tablespoons *liquid* pectin

2 8-ounce jars [one is for jam, the other is for the macarons]

Directions:

Mash up the raspberries in a medium sized bowl with a fork or a potato masher.

Strain if you don't want the seeds.

Pour berries into a very large saucepan or pot [6-8 quarts in size]. The fruit will cover the bottom in a thin layer.

Turn the burner to high.

Add the sugar, stirring the ingredients.

Add the sliver of butter to break up foam.

When the mixture reaches a full rolling boil that doesn't stop even when stirred, add the pectin.

Once the pectin has been quickly added, allow to boil for 1 minute.

Turn off heat and remove from burner.

Pour into glass jars.

Wait about an hour or until cooled down. Pour half the amount into a pastry bag with a large round tip.

Raspberry Buttercream Filling

Raspberry buttercream filling made with fresh raspberries.

Raspberry Buttercream Filling

Ingredients:

4 ounces unsalted softened butter [120 grams]

1 ¼ cups presifted powdered sugar/confectioners' sugar/icing sugar [156 grams]

4 ounces fresh raspberries [110 grams]

1 Tablespoon heavy cream

1 teaspoon vanilla bean paste

3 drops pink gel colorant [optional]

Directions:

Beat softened butter on medium speed for about 3-4 minutes until completely smooth and creamy. Add powdered sugar, cream, vanilla extract and raspberries with the mixer running. Increase to high speed and beat until thick and creamy, about 5 full minutes, so it's very soft and fluffy.

Blueberry Jam Filling

Blueberry jam with a fresh blueberry in the center.

Blueberry Jam Filling

Ingredients:

8 ounces fresh blueberries [220 grams]

1 ¾ cups granulated sugar/white sugar [350 grams]

Sliver unsalted butter

1 1/2 Tablespoons *liquid* pectin

2 8-ounce jars [one is for jam, the other is for the macarons]

Directions:

Mash up the blueberries in a medium sized bowl with a fork or a potato masher.

Pour berries into a very large saucepan or pot [6-8 quarts in size]. The fruit will cover the bottom in a thin layer.

Turn the burner to high.

Add the sugar, stirring the ingredients.

Add the sliver of butter to break up foam.

When the mixture reaches a full rolling boil that doesn't stop even when stirred, add the pectin.

Once the pectin has been quickly added, allow to boil for 1 minute.

Turn off heat and remove from burner.

Pour into glass jars.

Wait about an hour or until cooled down. Pour into a pastry bag with a large round tip.

Chocolate Ganache Filling

I used to think that a ganache was something fancy that went on top of a cake or some type of fancy pastry. I knew it was made from chocolate, but that's about all. If you've never made this lovely and decadent macaron filling, don't worry, it's very easy to make. You only need a few ingredients but you should get the best type of chocolate that you find appealing. For practice, use standard dark chocolate morsels that you may have in your pantry, but if you're a chocoholic, add a 70% cacao content dark chocolate.

Chocolate Ganache Filling

Ingredients:

1/2 cup heavy cream [120 grams]

3.5 ounces 70% cacao content chocolate [100 grams]

1 Tablespoon unsalted butter

½ teaspoon vanilla extract

Directions:

In a glass container, microwave cream for 1 minute until hot -- NOT boiling. Pour over chocolate chunks. When halfway melted add butter and vanilla and whisk well until smooth. Chill in fridge until paste consistency, about 30 minutes. Add to pastry bag and pipe it.

Double Cherry Buttercream Filling

Chunks of tart cherries from a natural spread and maraschino cherry bits

Double Cherry Buttercream Filling

Ingredients:

3/4 cup softened butter [170 grams]

3 1/2 cups presifted powdered sugar/confectioners' sugar/icing sugar [438 grams]

1 Tablespoon heavy cream

1 ½ Tablespoons maraschino cherry juice

1 1/2 teaspoons vanilla extract or vanilla bean paste

1/4 cup cherry preserves [63 grams]

5 drops magenta color

Directions:

Beat softened butter on medium speed for about 3-4 minutes until completely smooth and creamy. Add the confectioners' sugar, cream, vanilla extract, and maraschino cherry juice. Increase to high speed and beat for 1 minute. Add the cherry preserves and colorant and beat until thick and creamy, about 5 full minutes, so it's very soft and fluffy.

Pink Peppermint Buttercream Filling

Pink Peppermint Buttercream Filling

Ingredients:

½ cup of softened butter [113 grams]

1 1/2 cups presifted powdered sugar/confectioners' sugar/icing sugar [188 grams]

2 Tablespoons heavy cream

A few drops peppermint essential oil OR 1/2 teaspoon peppermint extract

5 drops pink gel colorant

Directions:

Blend the softened butter with half of the powdered sugar. Add the cream and peppermint extract or essential oil. Gradually add the remaining powdered sugar until the filling is the desired consistency. Add the pink colorant.

TIP: Use green colorant for a natural peppermint color.

Key Lime Curd Buttercream Filling

Only 5 ingredients make this delicious and tangy Key Lime filling.

Key Lime Curd Buttercream Filling

Ingredients:

1/4 cup softened unsalted butter [60 grams]

1 1/4 cup presifted powdered sugar/confectioners' sugar/icing sugar [156 grams]

5 Tablespoons key lime curd [70 grams]

1 teaspoon vanilla bean paste

10 drops green gel colorant [optional]

Directions:

Blend the softened butter with half of the powdered sugar. Add the key lime curd and vanilla. Gradually add the remaining powdered sugar until the filling is the desired consistency.

Tangy Orange Buttercream Filling

Tangy orange Buttercream Filling

Ingredients:

1/4 cup unsalted softened butter [60 grams]

1 1/2 cups presifted powdered sugar/confectioners' sugar/icing sugar [188 grams]

3 Tablespoons fresh tangelo or orange juice

½ teaspoon orange extract or a few drops sweet orange essential oil

1 teaspoon vanilla bean paste

7 drops orange gel colorant

Directions:

Blend the softened butter with half of the powdered sugar. Add the tangelo juice and vanilla. Gradually add the remaining powdered sugar until the filling is the desired consistency. Use either orange essential oil or orange extract and add a small amount, increasing if needed. Adding orange colorant is optional.

Note: you can use naval orange or use clementine, tangelo, tangerine, mandarin, blood orange, or yuzu.

Coconut Buttercream Filling

I was going to use some lemon curd and mix it with coconut extract but decided against it. McCormick's coconut extract was used and as a fan of anything coconut, I find it tastes a lot like fresh coconut. You can add a dollop of lemon curd in the center of each pillow of coconut buttercream.

Coconut Buttercream Filling

Ingredients:

½ cup softened butter at room temperature [113 grams]

2 1/4 cups presifted powdered sugar/confectioners' sugar/icing sugar [288 grams]

2 Tablespoons heavy cream

1 Tablespoon vanilla bean paste

1 1/2 teaspoons coconut extract

Directions:

Blend the softened butter with half of the powdered sugar. Add the cream, vanilla and coconut extract. Gradually add the remaining powdered sugar until the filling is the desired consistency.

Chocolate Espresso Ganache Filling

Chocolate Espresso Ganache Filling

Ingredients:

4 ounces heavy cream [120 grams]

4 ounces finely chopped dark chocolate [120 grams]

½ teaspoon vanilla extract or vanilla bean paste

½ teaspoon instant espresso

Put cream in microwave for about one minute until hot -- NOT boiling. Pour over chocolate chunks. When melted add instant coffee and vanilla and whisk well until smooth. Let sit at room temperature for at least four hours or overnight. Cover with plastic wrap. Just before getting ready to use a spatula to scoop the ganache into a piping bag with large round tip.

This is a simple recipe to make and it will really perk up your macaron shells. The touch of espresso gives the chocolate more zing! I used my favorite brand: Valrhona.

Chocolate Mint Ganache

Chocolate Mint Ganache

Ingredients:

4 ounces heavy cream [120 grams]

4 ounces mint chocolate [120 grams]

1 teaspoon vanilla bean paste

½ teaspoon peppermint extract or a few drops peppermint essential oil

Directions:

Chop up the chocolate and place in a medium glass bowl. Put heavy cream in a glass container and set microwave timer for 50 seconds. It should be on the verge of boiling. Pour hot cream over chocolate chunks that are in a glass bowl. Whisk both ingredients together a few times. Add the vanilla bean paste and peppermint EO. Cover with cling wrap and let sit overnight. The next day, mix once more and spoon into a piping bag.

The following photo of the chocolate mint ganache shows it the next day after it was sitting in a cupboard overnight, covered in cling wrap. All I did was mix it with a silicone spatula a couple of times.

Caramel Filling

Just poured caramel filling

Caramel Filling Recipe

Ingredients:

½ cup heavy cream [135 grams]

½ cup water [125 grams]

1 cup granulated sugar [210 grams]

1/3 cup room temperature cubed butter [80 grams]

Directions:

In a heavy-duty pot, add sugar and water together. Your stovetop temperature should be low.

Don't stir even when it's bubbling and before it turns brown.

CHAPTER 9

The Recipe Guide

As a writer, it's natural for me to take notes. The following recipe guide may seem excessively detailed or maybe it's not detailed enough, that's for you to decide. I didn't intend to take extensive notes as I only planned to make one batch of macarons. Then I decided to try another batch, and another. Each time, I'd write notes and it just grew into a habit.

By the way, before I ever referred to each recipe as a batch, I used the word attempt. After a few tries I decided I was doing more than attempting to bake macarons, they really were batches!

Before you begin, please do an ingredients checklist. Make certain you have all the ingredients and necessary equipment. I once spent 45-minutes hunting for an oven thermometer! My first batch was delayed by a few hours after realizing the sieve I was using was too fine, so I had to go to the store and buy a larger size.

♥ Date

♥ Name/flavor of macaron recipe

♥ Batch number [optional]

♥ Sift/process almond flour

♥ Start meringue

♥ Time of frothy texture

♥ Time of soft peaks

♥ Time when adding cream of tartar and/or salt

♥ Time when adding first part of granulated sugar

♥ Time when adding second part of granulated sugar

♥ Time when adding third part of granulated sugar

♥ Time when meringue has reached stiff peak [north star]

♥ Note if you're adding color and what type [gel, liquid or powder]

♥ Time when beginning macaronage process

♥ Number of strokes before adding second half of flour/sugar mixture [if counting]

♥ When piping: note the time you started piping each tray

♥ Count the number of shells on each tray

♥ Set oven temperature [if you haven't already done so]

♥ Make filling

♥ Once your macarons have rested, make sure they're done and add the first baking sheet

♥ Note the oven temperature and the time

♥ About halfway through baking, rotate the tray

♥ Check the oven temperature to see if it's changed

♥ When the shells are done, put on cooling rack and rest for about 10 minutes

♥ Check oven temperature before adding the second tray

♥ Remove macaron shells from first tray and place on wax paper covered flat surface

Summary checklist:

♥ Mix and measure ingredients

♥ Whip meringue

♥ Macaronage

♥ Pipe macaron shells

♥ Bake macaron shells

♥ Make filling

♥ Remove macaron shells from trays, match pairs and fill

♥ Store in a tightly sealed container in your refrigerator

CHAPTER 10

Resources

Where do you get your ingredients and supplies? That answer will mostly like be your supermarket, department store or online specialty shop.

Almond flour ~
http://www.kingarthurflour.com/shop/items/almond -flour-1-lb

Bob's Red Mill super-fine almond flour from blanched whole almonds ~
http://www.bobsredmill.com/almond-meal-flour.html

Amazon link: https://www.amazon.com/Bobs-Red-Mill-Super-Fine-16-ounce/dp/B010NBN1TM

Other brands of almond flour

Amazon:
https://www.amazon.com/s/ref=nb_sb_noss_2?url=se arch-alias%3Daps&field-keywords=finely+ground+almond+flour

Sugar

Finely ground sugar/caster sugar ~
https://www.amazon.com/s/ref=nb_sb_noss_1?url=se arch-alias%3Daps&field-keywords=caster+sugar

Powdered sugar/icing sugar ~
https://www.dominosugar.com/sugar/confectioners-sugar

Colorants Confection Crafts colorant ~
http://confectioncrafts.com/shop/natural-
colors/natural-powder-colors.html

Lorann Food coloring powder ~
https://www.amazon.com/Lorann-Coloring-Powder-
Ounce-Colors/dp/B006XJCG0O

Wilton neon gel food colors
https://www.amazon.com/Wilton-Neon-Gel-Food-
Color/dp/B007EMYD8M

Bakeware

Cookie Sheets

https://www.amazon.com/Farberware-Nonstick-
Bakeware-11-Inch-17-Inch/dp/B00008W70E

http://www.wilton.com/17x11-jelly-roll-pan/2105-
968.html#start=6

NOTE: Whether a jelly roll pan or a cookie sheet is
used, please remember to cover it with a silicone mat
OR parchment paper!

Parchment Paper

https://www.amazon.com/Kirkland-Signature-Stick-
Parchment-Paper/dp/B006JCWGIC

Silicone Mats

Amazon Basics
https://www.amazon.com/AmazonBasics-Silicone-Baking-Mat-Pack/dp/B00V5IM0EU

Velesco

https://www.amazon.com/Silicone-Baking-Mat-Professional-Nonstick/dp/B00Y5VO6HS

Simple Baker Premium Silicone Baking Mat for Macarons

https://www.amazon.com/Simple-Baker-Premium-Silicone-Macarons/dp/B015MMI9EE

Digital Scales

https://www.amazon.com/Digital-Kitchen-Scales/b?ie=UTF8&node=678508011

Liquid Pectin

Can be found in the baking aisle or the canning section in your supermarket

Vanilla Bean Paste

http://www.nielsenmassey.com/consumer/products-madagascar-bourbon-pure-vanilla-bean-paste.php

Wilton disposable 16-inch bags
https://www.amazon.com/Wilton-Disposable-16-Inch-Decorating-Bags/dp/B00175TFJ4/ref=pd_sim_79_2?ie=UTF8&psc=1&refRID=DF3GPH07K8AXY5BZHVFW

Wilton tips – this is a 4-pack of large tips which includes 2 round and 2 star tips. This was the original set I bought to get started.

https://www.amazon.com/dp/B00FGVD8UW/ref=psd
c_13825881_t1_B0043UJERS

Wilton Industries
http://www.wilton.com

Other stores with baking supplies:

Bed Bath & Beyond
https://www.bedbathandbeyond.com

Hobby Lobby

http://www.hobbylobby.com

Jo-Ann Fabric and Crafts Stores
http://www.joann.com

Michaels Arts & Crafts

http://www.michaels.com

Sur la Table

http://www.surlatable.com

Williams-Sonoma

http://www.williams-sonoma.com

CHAPTER 11

Recommended Books, Websites & Videos

Books:

Macarons: Authentic French Cookie Recipes from the Macaron Café by Cecile Cannone

https://www.amazon.com/Macarons-Authentic-French-Recipes-Macaron-ebook/dp/B004DNWBYI

Les Petits Macarons: Colorful French Confections to Make at Home by Kathryn Gordon & Anne E. McBride

https://www.amazon.com/Petits-Macarons-Colorful-French-Confections-ebook/dp/B005QBKXQO

Mad about Macarons!: Make Macarons like the French by Jill Colonna

https://www.amazon.com/Mad-about-Macarons-Make-French-ebook/dp/B00V2K2ZZK/#nav-subnav

Macaron Magic by Jialin Tian

https://www.amazon.com/Macaron-Magic-Jialin-Tian-ebook/dp/B00634F034#nav-subnav

Macarons: Chic and Delicious French Treats by Annie Rigg

https://www.amazon.com/Macarons-Chic-delicious-french-treats-ebook/dp/B00J75NDBW#nav-subnav

I Love Macarons by Hisako Ogita

https://www.amazon.com/I-Love-Macarons-Hisako-Ogita-ebook/dp/B00B2XPBLW#nav-subnav

Macarons Math, Science, and Art by Paula Ann Lujan Quinene

https://www.amazon.com/Macarons-Science-Paula-Lujan-Quinene-ebook/dp/B00C01JKBC#nav-subnav

The Quick Start Guide to Macarons: The Secrets to Baking Amazing Macarons Revealed Step-By-Step (Recipes Made Simple, Macarons) by Lindsay Stotts

https://www.amazon.com/Quick-Start-Guide-Macarons-Step-ebook/dp/B00IWTYTE4#nav-subnav

Making Macarons: What Recipes Don't Tell You by Julia C and Tania C.
https://www.amazon.com/gp/product/B0076UT8Y6

Macarons for the American Kitchen by Connie Finkelman

https://www.amazon.com/Macarons-American-Kitchen-Connie-Finkelman-ebook/dp/B008ZHY4WA/

Pierre Herme Macarons: The Ultimate Recipes from the Master Patissier by Pierre Herme
https://www.amazon.com/Pierre-Herm%C3%A9-Macarons-Ultimate-P%C3%A2tissier/dp/1617691712/

Sweet Macarons: Delectable French Confections for Every Day by Mercotte

https://www.amazon.com/Sweet-Macarons-Delectable-French-Confections/dp/1600854990

Creative Baking: Macarons by Tan Phay Shing

https://www.amazon.com/Creative-Baking-Tan-Phay-Shing-ebook/dp/B01IF3NEZ6

Websites:

Indulge with Mimi~ She generously shares so much information about macarons and other sweets.

http://www.indulgewithmimi.com/correctly-using-your-home-oven-for-baking-macarons

Bravetart ~ Stella is a pastry chef who loves to bake and write about macarons. The following link leads to more than a dozen different articles.

http://bravetart.com/blog/macarons

Love and macarons ~ Natalie embarks on a journey to make the perfect macaron.

http://loveandmacarons.blogspot.com/

Not so Humble Pie ~ Macaron 101 ~ French Meringue
http://notsohumblepie.blogspot.com/2010/04/macarons-101-french-meringue.html

Article entitled "Of ovens and baking [and macarons]"

http://www.syrupandtang.com/201003/of-ovens-and-baking-and-macarons

Temperature Conversion Calculator

http://www.traditionaloven.com/conversions_of_measures/temperature_units.html

Conversion of Measurements

http://www.convertunits.com/from/grams/to/cups

Macaron Templates

I recommend either the second to the last one entitled "Macaron Template PDF" or the last one entitled "Free Macaron Template."

https://www.sampletemplates.com/business-templates/macaron-template.html

Videos:

The first macaron baking video I ever watched:

https://www.youtube.com/watch?v=f_kn2x1Qj4E

An updated version of same video and you'll see her progression as a baker!

https://www.youtube.com/watch?v=0JeTgZGt-p8

Joy of Baking ~ French Macarons Recipe Demonstration

https://www.youtube.com/watch?v=jR7lNITB7ZY

Tatyana's Everyday Food

Triple Strawberry Macarons with cup and gram measurements.

https://www.youtube.com/watch?v=NILuEFmoxNs

Blanch Turnip ~ Frank loves sweets and shares many macaron videos!

https://www.youtube.com/user/blanchturnip

CHAPTER 12
About the Author

Thank you for taking the time to read **Baking French Macarons: A Beginner's Guide**. Feel free to leave a review on Amazon. Also, tell your friends, family and local library about this book, along with any of my other titles!

Happy Baking!

Lisa Maliga is an American author of contemporary fiction, psychological thrillers and cozy mysteries. Her nonfiction titles consist of how to make bath and body products with an emphasis on melt and pour soap crafting. When researching her latest cozy mystery, she discovered the art of baking French macarons. She continues to bake macarons every week, always trying new flavor combinations.

When not writing, Lisa reads, watches movies, and is a huge fan of "The Walking Dead."

You'll find more about her work at:

http://www.lisamaliga.com

http://lisamaliga.wordpress.com

http://pinterest.com/lisamaliga

https://twitter.com/LisaMaliga

http://www.goodreads.com/LisaMaliga

FICTION:

**The Aroma of Love (The Yolanda's Yummery
Series, Book 3)** - This novel centers around Yolanda's
Yummery, Yolanda Carter's bakery in the trendy Los
Angeles suburb of Brentwood. A cold case of a much-
loved pie baker murdered in her home has turned up
no leads until Detective Winston Churchill takes on
the case, assisted by Yolanda.

**Boxed Set: The Yolanda's Yummery Series Books 1
to 3** - This collection of sweet romance/cozy mystery
eBooks contains 3 full-length novels plus a chapter to
the novella that started it all: Sweet Dreams. Best of
all, it's value priced!

Diary of a Hollywood Nobody - Chris Yarborough is a
Midwesterner as green as the corn back home in Ohio.
This former bookstore employee moves out to Los
Angeles to pursue a profitable career in screenwriting.

**The Great Brownie Taste-off (The Yolanda's
Yummery Series, Book 1)** - The first book in the
Yolanda's Yummery series. Yolanda Carter is a self-
taught baker who dreams of owning her own bakery,
a/k/a yummery. Employed at a small cat shelter, she
stumbles across a scheme that threatens all the
employees and cats. Will her magical brownies save

them? FREE in eBook format. Also available in paperback format.

Hollywood After Dark: 3 Tales of Terror – [Paperback and eBook] This trio of horror novelettes takes place in Los Angeles and Hollywood. Titles include: Satan's Casting Call, An Author's Nightmare, and Hollywood Starz Storage.

I Almost Married a Narcissist - Charlotte White falls in love with a younger Romanian gymnastics coach. Andrei Antonescu is a sexy and handsome foreigner who loves to have fun and flirt with the ladies. The more she gets to know him, the more red flags are unfurled. Once she's able to see past his good looks and muscular body, Charlotte is unprepared for some shocking revelations.

I WANT YOU: Seduction Emails from a Narcissist - Arlen J. Stevenson is a narcissist who uses his scant literary accomplishments to entice his online victims. Meeting and seducing vulnerable women is what drives this Alabama-born man. [Paperback and eBook]

Macarons of Love [The Yolanda's Yummery Series, Book 4] - Yolanda Carter is preparing for Valentine's Day as romance and macarons are baking in Yolanda's Yummery. But things take a dark turn when the body of someone she knows is found dead in a nearby dumpster.

Magical Cakes of Love [The Yolanda's Yummery Series, Book 2] - Yolanda's Yummery is off to a promising start with excellent reviews and many happy fans of the delicious desserts. An accompanying Beverage Bar will open in three weeks. Yolanda's involved in a budding romance with sophisticated British tea baron, Nigel Garvey. Life is sweet. Until a homeless customer disappears...and Yolanda becomes a suspect. [Paperback and eBook]

The Narcissist Chronicles: The WHOLE Story - Combined are the two narcissist novels: LOVE ME, NEED ME: A NARCISSIST'S TALE and I WANT YOU: SEDUCTION E-MAILS FROM A NARCISSIST.

North of Sunset - It's 1996 and Hollywood is thriving in the era of indulgences. Sherman Lee is a volatile and successful action movie producer who seeks critical acceptance. Ever the partier, his excesses are starting to take their toll. He can't keep a personal assistant more than a few days until Emily Karelin is sent to fill the position. She's a temp with no showbiz background, one of the requirements Sherman demands. [Paperback and eBook]

Out of the Blue - Sylvia Gardner is a naïve cashier who lives with her mother in Richport, Illinois. Upset with being dumped by her first boyfriend; she later falls in love with an English actor after watching him on a TV show. For two years, she researches Alexander Thorpe's life and career, saving her money to travel to his Cotswolds village, intent on meeting him. [Paperback and eBook]

Satan's Casting Call - Duncan Smith-Holmes is a struggling young actor who is in desperate need of a paying gig or he has to leave Hollywood.

South of Sunset - Such a world-renowned name conjures up images of movies, sunglass-wearing stars, palm trees, plastic surgery, drug habits, the proverbial overnight success ... and the happy ending. In this collection of original short fiction, the author takes us into the minds of an assortment of losers, dreamers, successes, wannabes, and has-beens.

Sweet Dreams - Brenda Nevins is a successful romance author with a movie deal, a reality TV show, and a forthcoming bakery. Complications arise whenever any communication she sends or receives turns into fragments of a science fiction story. Will she find whoever is responsible for hijacking her career, finances, and even her fiancé?

NONFICTION:

12 Easy Melt and Pour Soap Recipes - Contains original recipes, 37 color photos, and several places to buy soap base, molds, fragrances and other necessary supplies. Learn how easy it is to craft your own melt and pour soap in less than one hour!

Fun Foodie Soap Crafting - You'll receive more than a dozen original and tested recipes, pretty packaging and labeling tips, 40+ photos, mistakes to avoid, and numerous supplier resources.

Happy Birthday Melt and Pour Soap Recipes - Say Happy Birthday with hand crafted soap! This unique book contains eight recipes for all budgets, along with melt and pour information, and birthday soap presentation tips. Contains 30+ color photos.

How to Make Handmade Shampoo Bars – Learn how easy it is to make natural handmade shampoo bars. This innovative eBook includes 25+ recipes for shampoo bars, hair rinses, and hair masques. Contains more than 50 color photos, step-by-step instructions, and a chapter on natural additives.

How to Make Handmade Shampoo Bars: The Budget Edition [Paperback only] – Same as above only with black and white photos.

Is the Long Island Medium the Real Deal? [Editor] - In this groundbreaking book, author and demonologist Kirby Robinson examines Theresa Caputo's claims of mediumship and what's on The Other Side. [Paperback and eBook]

The Joy of Melt and Pour Soap Crafting is written by someone who learned how to work with crafting glycerin melt & pour soap the hard way -- with only a single page of instructions to follow! If you've always wanted to make your own soap, here's an opportunity to learn just how easy it really is! Contains 40 recipes and MUCH more!

Kitchen Soap for Chefs: 4 Easy Melt & Pour Soap Recipes - It's easy to create chef's soap in your kitchen. Quickly cook up a batch of soap that will wash away strong kitchen odors. Now you can make excellent smelling and deodorizing soaps with four classic and carefully tested recipes.

Liquid **African Black Soap Recipes for Skin and Hair** - Make your own liquid African black soap in minutes! Includes five easy recipes using natural ingredients. You also receive information about essential oils and where to buy links for African black soap and other healthy additives.

Maple Sugar Melt & Pour Soap Recipe FREE at Smashwords. Learn how to make a fun fall melt and pour soap recipe starring pure maple syrup—a healthy addition.

Matcha Green Tea Melt & Pour Soap Recipe – Learn how easy it is to make this luxurious melt and pour soap starring Matcha Green Tea. This soap is wonderful for all skin types. It would make a great addition to any bath and body or tea lover's gift basket! FREE eBook.

Monoi de Tahiti: Spa in a Bottle - What is Monoi de Tahiti and how will it benefit you? A bottle of this Polynesian beauty product has a variety of uses and will soothe your skin, hair, and nails. "Monoi de Tahiti: Spa in a Bottle" is a unique e-book focused on this fragrant and natural Tahitian beauty oil.

MORE Joy of Melt and Pour Soap Crafting - Two eBooks in one! You get *The Joy of Melt and Pour Soap*

Crafting and *12 Easy Melt and Pour Soap Recipes* in one volume!

Nature's Beauty Oils: Monoi de Tahiti and Shea Butter – Two eBooks in one! Learn about nature's most versatile beauty oil and butter.

Never Mock God: An Unauthorized Investigation into Paranormal State's "I Am Six" Case - *Paranormal State*'s "I Am Six" episode is a perfect American horror tale -- for all the wrong reasons. It stars the ambitious founder of the Paranormal Research Society, an attention-seeking client, a bumbling group of paranormal investigators, a psychic-medium in search of ratings, and a rogue exorcist. [Paperback and eBook]

Nilotica [East African] Shea Body Butter Recipes [The Whipped Shea Butter Series], Book 1 - Learn the quickest and easiest way to whip Nilotica shea butter. Each recipe is easy to follow and includes the time it takes and amount it yields. Find out the secret to getting that incredibly light and airy texture.

Nuts About Shea Butter - The reader will discover shea butter's benefits, its numerous applications, and how to get optimal use from this healthy and natural nut fat. Learn about the differences between East African and West African shea butter. See photos of the various types of shea butter.

Organic and Sulfate Free Melt and Pour Glycerin Soap Crafting Recipes - If you want to make the most natural soap without using lye, here is a way to craft organic and sulfate free melt and pour glycerin soap at home. In less than an hour, you can craft lovely organic, sulfate free and eco-friendly Castile soaps with these carefully tested recipes.

Paranormal State Exposed [Co-Author] - Explore the rumors of staged scenes, questionable evidence, misleading editing, and duped clients. As other paranormal programming comes along imitating this style of presentation, it's vital that the problems are investigated.

Paranormal State: The Comprehensive Investigation [Co-Author] - Includes the eBooks *Paranormal State Exposed* and *Never Mock God: An Unauthorized Investigation into Paranormal State's "I Am Six" Case.*

The Prepper's Guide to Soap Crafting and Soap Storage - Be the cleanest prepper around! Create your own lye-free soap or find the best type of soap to store in the coming years. Informative book shows the best ways to craft your own soap. You'll receive original recipes and valuable storage tips to get the most out of your soap.

Rooibos Tea and Pink Kaolin Shampoo Bar Recipe - Discover how to craft rebatch/hand-milled soap base into a unique and versatile shampoo bar for most hair types. Also includes a recipe for Rooibos tea and apple cider vinegar hair rinse.

The Soapmaker's Guide to Online Marketing – This handy eBook is packed with detailed information on designing, building, and promoting your website. Learn how to write a press release. Get loads of free promotional ideas. Learn easy search engine optimization techniques and much more.

Squirrels in the Hood - When Sunshine the cat departs in 2006, the second story balcony she occupied is very empty. Now that birds can be fed, the author does so, also attracting an array of hungry squirrels.

Vanilla Bean Melt & Pour Soap Recipe - Learn how easy it is to make this creamy melt and pour soap with natural vanilla beans. This type of soap is wonderful for all skin types and would make an excellent addition to any bath & body gift basket! FREE eBook.

Made in United States
North Haven, CT
03 November 2022

26256580R00074